SWEATSHIRTS

By Debra Quartermain

©2007 by Debra Quartermain
Published by

krause publications
An Imprint of F+W Publications

700 East State Street • Iola, WI 54990-0001
715-445-2214 • 888-457-2873
www.krausebooks.com

Our toll-free number to place an order or obtain a free catalog is (800) 258-0929.

The following trademarked terms and companies appear in this publication:

Clover, Kandi Corp Crystal Crafter®, Kreinik, Janome Canada, Fiskars®, Ott Lite®, Polarfleece®, Therm O Web HeatnBond® Iron-on Adhesive

Library of Congress Catalog Number: 2006935751

ISBN-13: 978-0-89689-486-0

Illustration and Artwork by Deborah Peyton
Pattern Sheet by Charles Bliss
Designed by Rachael Knier
Edited by Erica Swanson

ACKNOWLEDGMENTS

When I taught kindergarten, I would always dress up for Halloween with the children. One year, I made a lacy lavender fairy godmother dress and wore it for our party (a couple of days before Halloween). I went to answer the door, wand in hand, and there stood the UPS guy. He didn't speak right away, but he went away with a big grin. That was just part of my fairy godmother career of waving a needle and scissors to make magic happen and transform fabrics and trims into clothing. From making doll clothes at age five under my mother's expert guidance, to stitching my own baby daughter's matching outfits, I have always loved sewing.

I turned my love of designing, sewing and teaching into a business. I love to design and sew, I love to teach and I love jackets, and it has all come together perfectly in this book!

My creativity has blossomed throughout my life. The seeds were lovingly planted by my parents and nurtured along the way by the love and support of my brother, Bob, my delightful daughters, Amanda and Kate, and the dearest of friends, Alison, Karen and Deborah. Several other close friends, Julie, Marie, Cheryl and Lorine have been part of my creative journey as well, and I am truly grateful for my joy-filled life, magic wand and all!

As always, everyone at Krause Publications makes each book a wonderful experience, from acquisitions editor Candy Wiza, who gave me this opportunity, to my editor Erica Swanson and designer Rachael Knier. A highlight of each book is the photo shoot, where I visit Krause and spend several delightful days. The models from Face Station Inc. wore the jackets with such style and showed them off wonderfully.

At home, I am fortunate to work with good friend and talented illustrator Deborah Peyton, who brought my vision for the book to life. Charles Bliss transformed my rough pattern pieces into an expert layout. Also, image consultant Diana Pemberton-Sykes has graciously contributed her expertise.

So, the fairy tale begins! Step inside with me to learn, laugh and love the fabulous jackets you will create from a simple sweatshirt.

— Debra

TABLE OF CONTENTS

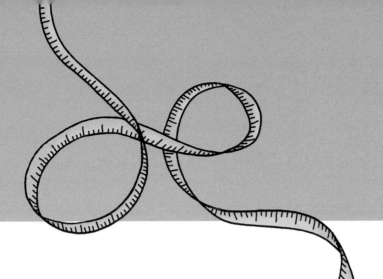

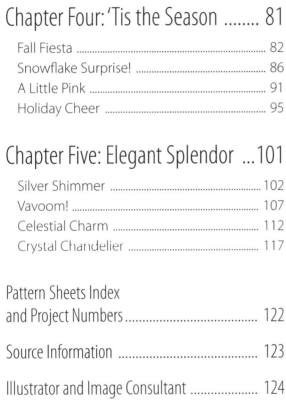

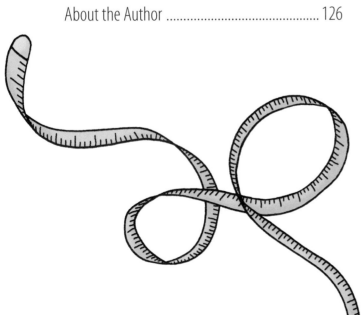

FOREWORD

Finding the best clothes for your body shape has been a problem for women since time began. While some lucky gals can get away with wearing just about anything, the majority of the population cannot. Some women have full busts and trim torsos, while others carry their weight in their hips. Still others are perfectly proportioned — but they're inches shorter than the rest of the population, making everything they buy either too big or too long.

So what's a girl to do to find clothes that fit correctly?

Adapt them to fit your needs.

Sewing is the easiest way to do this. Once you determine your body shape and which styles suit you best, you can tailor clothes to fit you properly and adapt trends to your proportions. Having trouble finding just what you want? Sew it! Sewing is a great way to build a wardrobe without the expense or time required to track down pieces that fit correctly.

So pay particular attention to these projects as you go through them. Before you know it, you'll have lots of snazzy, one-of-a-kind jackets that both look great and fit you properly.

If you work hard and are kind to others, you deserve every good thing that comes your way. Dressing appropriately all the time will help you get there. I guarantee it.

And who knows? Like Cinderella, you may even find yourself with an invitation to a ball — that's just the beginning of a whole new life.

Try it yourself and see!

— Diana Pemberton-Sikes
FashionForRealWomen.com

INTRODUCTION

The sweatshirt is a comfortable and warm staple in everyone's wardrobe. Available in basic gray and many other colors, a sweatshirt is the perfect blank canvas for transformation. "Sweatshirts" will show you how to embellish and alter sweatshirts into beautiful pieces of clothing alive with fabric, color and special details. You will learn techniques to create easy-to-wear and stylish blazers, coats, cardigans, beaded boleros, tunic jackets, short-sleeve jackets and three-quarter length jackets.

You can take the transformation one step further by creating jackets and vests that flatter your own unique shape and personality. Be comfortable and stylish by altering and restructuring different elements of the sweatshirt to fit the most common body types in the most attractive styles.

This book addresses three main female body types: the womanly round apple, the curvy bottom pear and the exquisite petite. Each chapter will feature garments that will work for individual body types, as well as tips on how to alter the jacket to flatter any body type. There are creative and striking designs to fit the many areas of your life, from work and play to evening and holiday. With the popularity of image makeover TV shows, women are becoming more aware of dressing to enhance their figures. "Sweatshirts" will show you how; and even more than that, this book is about celebrating your own personal style and dressing

the body you have. It is about feeling and looking great as you go about your full and busy life.

If you are interested in creating easy, stylish and unique garments, expanding your sewing repertoire with new skills that fit the time constraints of a busy lifestyle, and making a personal statement with a beautiful fashion piece, then this is the perfect book for you! There are many tips for successfully creating the designs in the book and wearing them with style. I am very pleased to have Diana Pemberton-Sykes, wardrobe and image consultant, contributing her expertise to this book.

So, celebrate your personal style and love what you wear! Take a couple of hours or an evening, grab some scissors, warm up your machine, wave your wand and make some great jackets!

CHAPTER ONE

LET'S DO IT!

DECISIONS, DECISIONS!

Your sewing adventure begins here with great tips and techniques to create stylish jackets with ease. You will find everything from choosing the best sweatshirts and fabric to cutting and construction techniques. As you choose the jackets you want to create, refer back to this chapter for all of the basic information. Easy, stylish, innovative and fabulous clothing begins now!

Your Body Type and Style

We all know if we are tall or petite, round through the middle or have larger hips. We all know what parts of our bodies we don't like, but more importantly, we all have lots of parts and lots to love! Make a list of your best features, including fingers and feet (anything you can accessorize definitely counts), and fit yourself into a general category below. There are many variations, but you will find one that is close to your body type, and then you will be able to choose or modify the jackets in the book to fit. It is really all about putting on a jacket and feeling wonderful wearing it!

Choosing Sweatshirt Size

While creating the designs for this book, I bought lots of sweatshirts and discovered there are many brands and fiber blends available. Sizes from brand to brand varied. Some brands are designed with a more fitted shape and shoulder. Traditional styling has a dropped shoulder and loose body shape for comfort, but adding simple structure details makes them comfortable AND stylish! Choose a sweatshirt brand that fits you well. For Petites, choose as fitted a brand as possible. For the Apple shape,

---

The Defining Body Types

Apple: Fuller bust and midsection area, often with narrow hips and thin legs.

Choose jackets that skim the body with vertical lines and shorter styles that elongate the legs. A V-neck makes this area appear longer and lets great cleavage peek out of a lace camisole. Three-quarter length sleeves show a little more skin, which is also flattering. Remember to skim the body, not swim in too-large jackets that only make the upper body look larger.

Pear: Smaller through the top half of the body with larger hips and legs.

Choose jackets that also have a vertical line and do not hit at the widest hip area. If you are tall, the longer three quarter jacket or coat is perfect, even shortened to hit a thinner part of the leg just below the thigh. A slightly flared style with a collar frames the face, and adding a soft shoulder pad helps balance out the body if you have narrow shoulders. Leave jackets and coats open to obtain the best vertical line. Dressing is easy — just remember to accent the positives: a waist, delicate upper body and attractive shoulders and arms.

Petite: Shorter than average (5'3" and under) with a small body frame.

Choose jackets of a shorter length like a bolero. Details and patterns should also be in proportion to body size.

look for fullness through the center of the sweatshirt. For the Pear shape, choose a sweatshirt that, when pulled down, will go over the top of the fuller hip area. If you are tall, check the length of the arms and body of the sweatshirt.

These measurements are guidelines for the projects in the book. Depending on the size of the sweatshirt you are using, the pattern pieces and seams can be adjusted for the best fit. Every jacket gives the size sweatshirt used and suggestions for altering it for other sizes and body types. Choose a sweatshirt that is the right size for your arm and body length, and fits comfortably through the middle. Then, measure the sweatshirt you are using and compare it to this chart.

Most neckbands are identical in size, so collars will fit without any adjustments. There are probably very few pattern pieces that will need adjusting. A dress form comes in handy, or you can just pin as you go along and try the jacket on inside out at various stages in the sewing process. A full-length mirror installed in your sewing area is very handy for checking how the jacket looks from all angles — and it curbs snacking (chocolate doesn't count, of course)!

Choosing the Blend and Color

Different brands of sweatshirts have different blends. Most sweatshirts are made of breathable and comfortable 100-percent cotton. This blend works well with many of the designs that use cotton fabrics. Cotton can shrink, so wash both the sweatshirt and fabrics before creating the jacket.

Many sweatshirts come pre-washed with a vintage finish, and these work well with a cardigan-style jacket, whereas a blend may work better for a dressy jacket. Other blends are 50-percent cotton and 50-percent man-made fibers, like polyester. These blends combine the characteristics of cotton with the ease of care of polyester. Polyester holds its shape, and it can be machine-washed and dried without shrinkage. There are other blends available as well. The one you choose is a matter of personal preference.

Last, but certainly not least, is the exciting range of colors available. I do not shop for sweatshirts too often, and I certainly have not ever done so on the large scale I did for this book, but it was exciting to visit an outlet and see a wall of colored sweatshirts. My daughter and friend were piled high with a rainbow of colors as they carried my selections. If you don't know which colors work for you, ask a friend or two to see what looks good when you hold various colors close to your face. I chose rich shades and stayed away from the super-bright colors. A splash of bright color in an accessory is fine, but a complete jacket in hot pink can be overwhelming. However, it is all about personal choice, and if you love that neon green or bright orange, then choose it for one of the casual jackets in Chapter Three, "Girls Just Want to Have Fun!" And with that cue, on to the fun stuff!

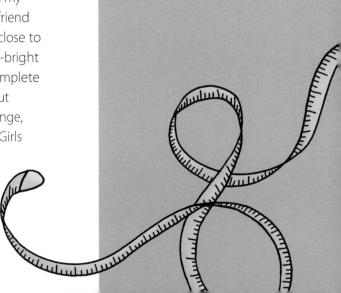

FABRIC-LICIOUS!

I have been shopping at our local fabric and quilt store for 20 years. It has expanded into a beautiful place for fabrics and trims for every sewing project imaginable. The inspiring displays throughout the store just add to the enjoyment of shopping, and the staff is always very friendly and helpful. I found everything I needed there, from fleece to batiks.

Choosing Fabric

Before shopping for fabrics, think about the design and the sweatshirt color and blend you are using. Next, consider your body type and the size of the pattern to use in proportion to your size.

Depending on the jacket, certain fabrics will be more casual and others will be dressier. Cottons work well with quilting details. Don't forget to shop the fat quarters and remnants, because several designs do not require large amounts of fabric. If you are going to make a jacket with reverse appliqué, like "A Touch of the Orient," pg. 43, choose a fabric that is dyed through both right and wrong sides, because you need to be able to see the design from the wrong side. Also in that design, I chose a beautiful embroidered fabric accent piece, which I embroidered even more.

Polarfleece for outerwear is easy to sew in combination with sweatshirt material. There are many types and qualities of fleece available; choose a medium-weight fleece with a non-pill finish. Sometimes it is hard to tell which is the right side of the fleece, but pulling along the selvage edge will curl it to the right side. You can also line the jacket with flannel for extra warmth. Another option is to shop for vintage garments with unusual fabric pieces to cut and use.

Wash your fabrics and sweatshirts before beginning a project, especially if the jacket will be worn frequently. If you love a fabric that is delicate or can't be laundered, consider making the jacket with detachable collar and cuffs. Several of the jackets in this book are designed with that possibility; check in the "Alter" section at the end of each project. Jackets for work and evening will not be worn as frequently, and professional cleaning could be an option — so don't bypass a fabric you just have to have!

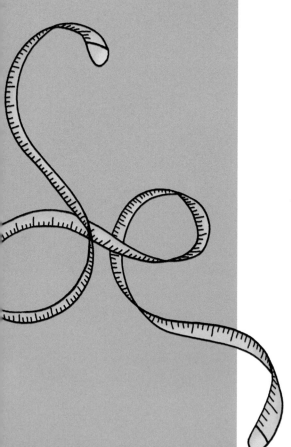

TRIMTATIONS!

Choosing Trims

There are so many trim and embellishment options that it may be hard to pick just one! Choosing can be overwhelming, so use your jacket design as a guide. You may decide to re-create the design using your own color choices. Create a rough sketch, and attach sweatshirt color samples and fabric swatches. Look for trims, ribbons, yarns and button closures that coordinate with your sketch. With these details, you can make a stylish and unique statement. Have fun experimenting with a variety of beautiful trims as well! Gorgeous fashion yarns and fibers can be used not only for knitted collars and cuffs, but also for creating one-of-a-kind details.

In "For the Animal in You," pg. 73, yarn was used to create a loopy collar and closures. The trim matches the velvet animal print perfectly!

Iron-on decorative threads and braid can also give the sweatshirt jacket a unique look. The "Vavoom!" blazer in Chapter Five combines decorative threads and braid with reverse appliqué. Kreinik has wonderful array of these specialty trims to create an instant embroidered look, and Clover's mini iron makes application easy. Bindings and ribbons can be used to outline seam lines, collars and hems, and satin ribbons make a beautiful belt. If you use trim for curves, make sure that you choose one that stretches or is cut on the bias. There are many bias-type trims that are perfect for edging, and you can also make your own from the fabric you use. The most important guideline is to choose good-quality trims and threads; this will be reflected in the polished look of your finished jacket.

Choose from yarns, ribbons and beaded trims.

Yarn creates an attractive collar and closures in this vest.

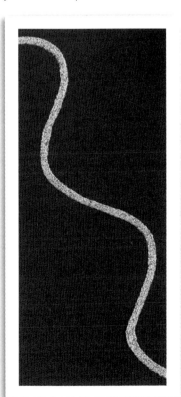

Iron-on braid

Choosing Closures

There are so many buttons, clasps, toggles and snaps from which to choose! Usually, you should save these details for last — but sometimes I just can't help myself!

One day I was perusing the notions aisles and I saw a gorgeous clasp. I just had to use it, and that one little clasp ended up inspiring an entire jacket idea. So go for whatever sparks your interest! You can choose something similar to what is used in the design (it should match your color and fabric, of course), or you can let your imagination run wild. You never know what will happen!

Vintage buttons are beautiful, and it's fun to hunt them down to complete a one-of-a-kind jacket. For evening jackets, gold or silver is always appropriate. You can also create your own buttons with the many tools available for that purpose, or fashion them from fabric as I did in Chapter Three with "Attitude Plus."

I liked the fabric, so I took large, plain buttons and decoupaged fabric to the buttons for a custom finish. Making buttonholes is easy, but if you choose a large button for its look, you might just want a couple of decorative buttons near the top and close the jacket farther down with large snaps on the inside. You can also use colored zippers as a contrasting element on a more casual jacket.

Create custom buttons from fabric.

For everyday jackets, choose trims that will be able to withstand frequent washings. For jackets that will require professional cleaning, you can include other trims and closures. If you want to use something vintage or special, the safest solution is to remove the trim before cleaning.

BEADS AND BAUBLES

Sewing opens unlimited possibilities to use all kinds of wonderful materials, trims and products. It also gives the sewer a terrific individual wardrobe — plus an excuse to shop for hours in fabric, quilt and craft stores!

Beads and beaded trims are the jewelry of the garment. They complete the jacket with a special, final touch. Beaded trims come sewn onto a satin ribbon band, ready to be stitched in place by hand or machine. Be sure to pin or baste first, and use a regular presser foot to sew. Similar beads can be used to create designs elsewhere on the jacket. Beads are sold by the strand or in packages. Seed beads (about 1.4mm) and slightly larger E beads (4mm), as well as bugle and bicone beads, were used for some of the designs in this book.

The "Petite Play" jacket in Chapter Three is a good example of E beads being used to accent a border. I used a strong, durable thread (for quilting or upholstery) to sew them to the jacket. You can also use beading thread. Sew on just a few beads, or create an intricate design. Shop the aisles of your quilting or craft store for a wide selection of beads suitable for clothing.

You can create a glittering look with iron-on beads, rhinestones and studs, which can be used to fill in wide areas. I like the Kandi Corp. Crystal Crafter, which has a heated tip to attach rhinestones, studs and beads.

The tool heats the glue, resulting in a stunning sparkle in a few seconds.

Whether you buy or decide to do it yourself, just remember the rules of proportion: keep embellishments in proportion to your body size.

— Diana

HANDS ON!

To sew or not to sew? If time is an issue, there are tips to save minutes throughout the book, and you can always try machine quilting or embroidery. But if you prefer to hand-quilt a collar or crazy-quilt feature on a jacket, use the following embroidery stitches: blanket stitch, cross stitch, chain stitch, herringbone stitch and backstitch. These are also useful to incorporate when beading.

Blanket Stitch

Cross Stitch

Herringbone Stitch

Chain Stitch

Redwork/back Stitch

Sewing a Yo-Yo Flower

Step 1

1. Sew around the edge of a small fabric or knit circle.

Step 2

2. Pull threads tight.

Step 3

3. Sew to the garment, taking the thread over the top of the yo-yo at the north, south, east and west to create flower petals, always returning to the center of your flower.

Sewing a Ribbon Embroidery Rose

Ribbon roses are easy to create, and it is satisfying to watch them take shape on a garment. Silk ribbon is often used for embroidery, but other ribbons also work well. This rose was created with a ¼" silver polyester ribbon, used in the "Crystal Chandelier" coat, Chapter Five.

1. Cut an 18" length of ribbon. Thread a crewel needle with the ribbon. To maximize use of the ribbon, take the point of the needle through the end of the ribbon before threading. This will hold the ribbon in place.

Step 2

2. Thread another needle with two strands of matching floss. Sew a straight stitch in the shape of a star on the garment, making each stitch approximately ½" long.

Step 3

A grouping of ribbon roses creates a stunning accent.

3. Knot a ribbon at the back of the star. Bring the ribbon up, and loop it in and out through the star. Twisted ribbon will add to the rose. Pull the ribbon gently.
4. Continue until the rose is finished, adding more ribbon from the back, if needed.

TOOLS RULE

The right tools help make the sewing experience easy and enjoyable, and I have listed those that were extremely useful for this book. Most of them are basic, essential tools for your sewing area.

1. Sewing machine: For the designs in this book, use a machine that has a variety of stitches, including the straight, zigzag and buttonhole stitch. (I love my Janome, which Janome Canada so generously gave me.) A serger for finishing seams comes in handy, and you can also use a small zigzag stitch. Machine embroidery can be used to embellish many of the jackets as well.

2. Cutting mat, rotary cutter and wide ruler: These are helpful for cutting fabrics and straightening sweatshirt edges. Fiskar's brand tools are my preference.

3. Scissors in different sizes: Use small, sharp-pointed scissors for reverse appliqué.

4. Iron and mini iron: Pressing every step will give you the best results. A mini iron is perfect for small details, like pressing seams and iron-on threads in place.

5. Pins and needles: I prefer the long quilters' pins with the colored heads. They are easy to put in and pull out, and the contrasting colors show up well against the fabrics. Several types of needles are good for these projects: sewing machine needles, universal 70 or 80 needles that work well with fleece, and size 22 embroidery needles.

6. Hot-fix crystal applicator: This tool affixes crystals, rhinestones and studs in seconds as it holds and heats the crystal. Then, just press them in place.

7. Quilter's pencil and/or chalk: Use these to draw pattern lines and mark details for cutting and sewing.

8. Fusible products, interfacing and quilt batting: These are excellent for fusing and stabilizing hems, especially HeatnBond Iron-on Adhesives in sheets and tapes. Interfacing and lightweight quilt batting give collars and cuffs body.

9. Lighting: Ott-Lites provide excellent light for working on small details.

Cutting Basics

Each jacket or vest has detailed step-by-step cutting instructions, and there are some general basic cuts used often throughout the book. Refer back to this section when needed.

Cut the ribbed band from your sweatshirt.

1. To remove the bottom band, cut close to the stitching lines. Cut off cuffs close to the stitching lines. The neckband can be removed in the same manner, but many of the designs keep this as a collar.

Cut the underarm seams open close to the stitch line.

2. Turn the sweatshirt inside out, and cut carefully along the underarm seams. If the sweatshirt does not have an underarm seam, draw a chalk line from the underarm and cut along this line. It is easy to work on the jacket once you lay it completely flat.

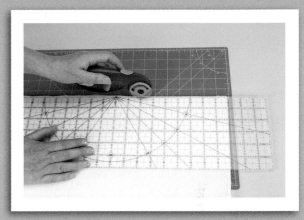

Straighten and cut all the edges easily with the sweatshirt lying flat.

3. Lay the sweatshirt flat, and use a mat, rotary cutter and ruler to straighten edges and cut the specified measurements from the bottom of your sweatshirt.

Measure and cut sleeves off ½" beyond the seam line for a vest.

4. For vests, cut ½" beyond the shoulder seam line. For three-quarter length sleeves, cut arms with a rotary cutter at the specified measurement.

Mark and cut the center fold of your sweatshirt.

5. Measure and cut the center fold with a ruler and rotary cutter. From this point, make other cut variations according to the individual instructions and pattern pieces.

Cutting with Pattern Guides

For many of the jackets, use the simple pattern guides found in the book to cut neck and hem lines. Use the pattern guides as they are, or trace or glue them onto cardstock-weight paper. Many of the pattern guides are used in several jackets, so you may use them over and over. Place the thick pattern pieces in position on the flat jacket, trace with chalk, and then cut easily.

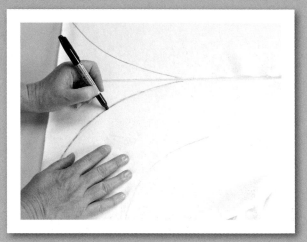

Place the guide along the lower edge of the sweatshirt, and draw the curve.

1. Lay the sweatshirt flat, wrong-side up, and place the curve pattern guide along the front lower edge. Draw around the curve. Repeat for the opposite curve.

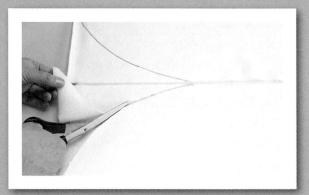

Cut along the curved line.

2. Cut along the curved line carefully, and repeat for the opposite front, making sure that the curves line up. Use the same method to cut the upper curve lines. The instructions will indicate which guide to use.

MACHINE MAGIC

Sewing terms used throughout the book:

1. **Seam:** Sew two separate pieces right-sides together with a ½"-wide sewing line, unless otherwise indicated.

2. **Finish seam:** After sewing the seams, trim to ¼" and serge or use a small zigzag stitch to finish.

3. **Stay-stitch:** Stitch inside the seam allowance before sewing the garment to stabilize the stretch of the sweatshirt; stay-stitching is usually done on a single thickness at ¼" width.

4. **Stitch in the ditch:** Stitch on the right side through a seam to hold the layers together and make them lie in the proper position.

5. **Topstitch:** Sew a ¼"-wide line of stitching, which will show on the top of the fabric. It can be decorative or functional.

This section covers basic sewing construction techniques used in many of the jackets and vests. Unless otherwise instructed, begin by stay-stitching ¼" around all of the edges; this will help stabilize the sweatshirt shape. Because sweatshirt fabric is stretchy, it may appear to be distorted while you are sewing. A thorough steam press will return the desired shape. Repeat if necessary. It is important to press thoroughly with every step, because this will give the finished jacket a polished appearance. The individual step-by-step instructions will refer you back to a specific technique when necessary. Included in this section are: Curved C Seam, Collars, Cuffs, Side Seams, Front Trim Binding and Shoulder Pads.

Curved Seam

The Curved C is one of the most flattering shapes in a garment structure. It adds an hourglass shape and vertical detail to the jacket. The Curved C is very similar to a princess seam (darts that start at the waist and goes over the bust), but here it is adapted to the sweatshirt structure.

Line up the Curve C guide along the sleeve stitch line.

1. Lay the jacket or vest completely flat, wrong side facing up. Place the Curve C guide from the pattern sheet along the sleeve stitch line, and draw the line. Repeat for the opposite front and opposite sides of the back, or as instructions indicate. Some jackets have curved seams in the back only.

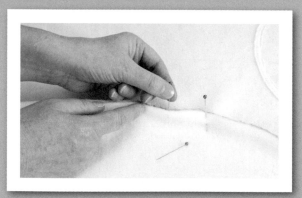

Fold along the curved line.

2. Right sides together, fold the sweatshirt along this line.

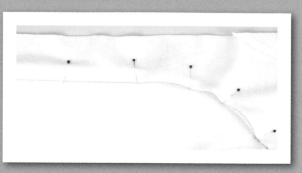

Mark and pin the sewing line.

3. Measure ¼" from the fold, and mark at the lower sweatshirt edge. Pin, narrowing (decreasing) to the seam at the opposite end. Sew along this line. Repeat for the remaining curves. The seam can be made larger, if needed, by adding another ¼" to the measurement and still narrowing to the sleeve seam.

Press curved C seam toward side seam.

4. Press all curved seams toward side seams.

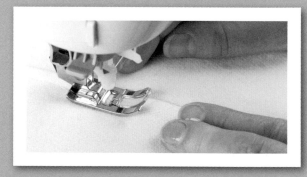

Topstitch seam.

5. Topstitch ⅛" from the seam on the right side of the sweatshirt, using matching or contrasting thread.

22

Collars

This collar application is very easy, and it produces a collar with a good shape.

Apply interfacing to the collar pieces.

1. Press interfacing to either side of the collar (use the correct pattern piece for your jacket). Pin interfaced collar pieces right sides together.

Sew seam allowance on all sides, leaving an opening.

2. Sew seam all around with ½" seam allowance unless otherwise indicated, leaving a 2" opening in the center top to turn.

3. Trim corners and seams. Turn and press.

4. Topstitch the collar ¼" from the edge on three sides. Use contrasting thread.

Pin the collar to the neck edge along the ribbing seam line.

5. Pin the right-side bottom edge of the collar to the wrong-side lower edge of neck ribbing.

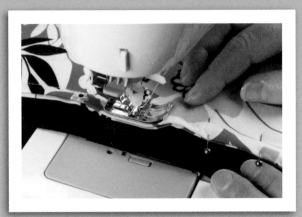

Sew the collar to the neck.

6. Sew along the bottom edge, using the topstitch line as a guide. Press seam.

Finish underneath the collar by stitching ribbing to underside of collar.

7. Flip the collar to the right side of the sweat-shirt jacket. Hand-stitch the ribbing to the collar lining.

Cuffs

There are several sleeve and cuff treatments. Some sleeves and cuffs are finished when the sleeve is flat, and others are finished after the jacket is sewn. This basic cuff with two fabrics is used in several jackets.

LONG-SLEEVE CUFFS

Step 1

1. Press interfacing to half of the wrong side of the two floral cuff pieces.

Step 2

2. Align pink cuff pieces to floral cuff pieces, right sides together.

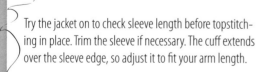

Try the jacket on to check sleeve length before topstitching in place. Trim the sleeve if necessary. The cuff extends over the sleeve edge, so adjust it to fit your arm length.

Step 3

3. Sew along both long sides, leaving a 2" opening to turn.
4. Press cuffs flat, with pink fabric centered at the top.
5. Sew along the short ends. Clip corners.
6. Turn and press.

Step 7

7. Press ½" to right side on end of sleeves.

Step 8

8. Pin cuffs to sleeve, extending over 2" from the sleeve end. The cuff ends will meet at the underarm seam. Topstitch in place.

24

Side Seams

This step is crucial to create a fitted and flattering hourglass-shaped jacket.

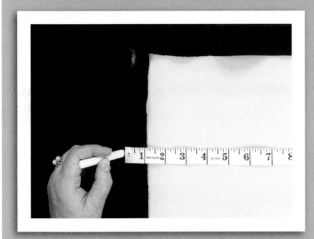

Mark 1" in at the center of the side seam line (black sweatshirt shown).

1. Fold your jacket right sides together along the underarm seam line. At the halfway point on the side seam, measure 1" in and mark.

Draw a line curving to ½" seam line.

2. From this point, draw a line gradually becoming ½" at either end of the seam, which is the regular seam width.

3. Pin along this line, and try the jacket on before continuing.

4. If the jacket is not fitted enough and the underarm is too wide, add another ¼" to your measurement, and redraw the line. If the jacket needs to be looser, reduce the line by ¼".

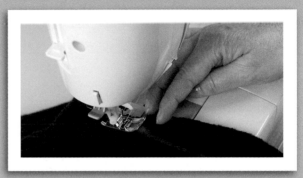

Sew seams along the drawn lines.

5. Sew seams.

6. Trim the excess from your seams to ¼" width, and finish with serging or a small zigzag stitch.

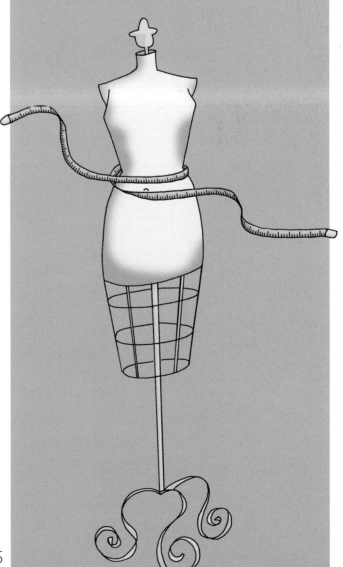

Front Trim Binding

Many jackets are finished with decorative fabric trim binding. Before cutting the trim, it is important to check the length of the sweatshirt. The front trim piece should be 1" longer than the sweatshirt front, including the neckband.

Press the trim in half to create front trim binding.

1. Press ½" under along each side of the two pieces of front trim. Press the top edges ½" under also. Fold the trim pieces in half, and press.

Insert the sweatshirt edge between the folds of trim.

2. Beginning at the top of the neckband, lay front trim in place and insert the sweatshirt edge between the folds of trim. Cut off the excess at the bottom, leaving ½" to press under. Pin in place, covering raw edges of the front.

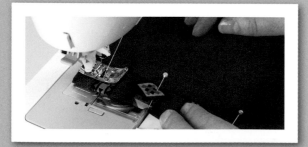

Topstitch in place.

3. Topstitch along the sides and ends of the front trim. Press.

Shoulder Pads

A soft shoulder pad is a way to add more shoulder definition, especially for women with narrow shoulders and sweatshirts with dropped shoulders. Fasten to the inside of the jacket with hook and loop squares. Hand-sew the hook piece to the inside of the jacket at the shoulder, and sew the loop piece to the top of the shoulder pad. A pattern is included on the Pattern Sheet.

Pin fabric pieces, right sides together, with lining pieces on one wrong side.

1. Use scraps of fabric to cut four fabric pieces on the fold. Cut two lining pieces from lightweight quilt batting. Pin fabric pieces right sides together, with lining pieces pinned to one wrong side.

Sew, leaving an opening to turn.

2. Sew around the shoulder pad, leaving a 2" opening to turn. Trim seams. Turn and press. Topstitch.

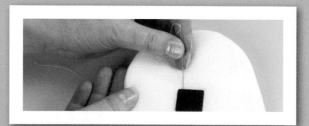

Sew the loop square centered on top of the shoulder pad.

3. Sew the loop square to the top of the shoulder pad.

CHAPTER TWO

The classic combination of black and white, along with a splash of color, showcases these easy-to-make and sophisticated jackets. Attention to accents, embellishment and detail will make your jacket stunning and smart. Start your day in style!

BLACK, WHITE AND WOW! ALL OVER

THE ACCENT IS ON YOU!

Hot pink punches up this three-quarter length jacket with detailed trim and stitching. Comfort and class are built into this striking design, sweatshirt bodice and A-line shape. In the office, wear with dress pants for professional flair. For an evening out, pair with a little black dress for a sophisticated dress coat ensemble. Either way, this jacket is easy to make and wear with head-turning style.

MATERIALS:

* 1 white sweatshirt
* 1½ yd. black, white and pink floral fabric
* ½ yd. pink fabric
* ¼ yd. interfacing
* ⅓ yd. ¼" black trim
* 2 white 1" buttons
* Iron-on adhesive tape
* Matching thread
* Sewing notions listed in Chapter One

Finished Length: 36"

PATTERNS:
Collar and Curved C Guide pieces from the Pattern Sheet
"The Accent is on You!" is #1 on the Pattern Sheet

white Sweatshirt

cut along center front line

5"

cut along line

cut off cuffs

cut off band

Accent on YOU
3/4 Dress coat
Body Type: Tall Pear
White Sweatshirt: M
Double cuffs
Front Trim Accent

CUTTING PLAN

- ❋ Cut two 16" x 25" front pieces from floral fabric
- ❋ Cut one 26" x 25" back piece from floral fabric
- ❋ Cut two 3" x 38" front trim pieces from floral fabric
- ❋ Cut two 1½" x 38" front trim pieces from pink fabric
- ❋ Cut two 6" x 12½" cuff pieces from floral fabric
- ❋ Cut two 3½" x 12½" cuff trim pieces from pink fabric
- ❋ Cut two 3" x 12½" cuff pieces from interfacing
- ❋ Cut two 4" lapel squares from floral fabric
- ❋ Cut two 5" lapel squares from pink fabric
- ❋ Cut one upper collar from floral fabric
- ❋ Cut one under collar from pink fabric
- ❋ Cut one collar from interfacing
- ❋ Cut two 3" pieces of trim for loops

Reviewing Chapter One before you begin will be very helpful. Sew ½" seams with pieces right sides together, unless otherwise indicated.

Cutting the Sweatshirt

1. Refer to the Inspiration Board for the cutting diagram for your sweatshirt. Cut off the band and cuffs.

2. Cut the sweatshirt open along the underarm seams.

3. Measure 5" down from the underarm seams. Cut the sweatshirt off along this line.

4. Measure and cut open along the center front line.

Back of the jacket.

Cutting the Lower Jacket

1. Lay one floral jacket front piece flat, wrong sides up.

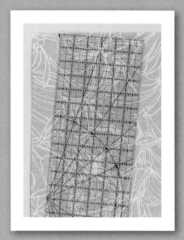

Step 2

2. Measure in 2" at the top of the piece on one outside edge, and mark.

Step 3

3. Line up the ruler from the bottom outside edge to the mark at the top.

4. Cut along this diagonal line for the side seam line.

Step 5

5. Use this front piece as a pattern guide for cutting the opposite front side seam and back side seam lines.

Sewing Jacket Pieces

1. Align the back pieces right sides together, pinning the lower jacket to the upper jacket. Sew seam. Finish the seam, and press.

2. Press ½" under along both of the front straight edges of the lower jacket. Topstitch.

3. Align the lower front pieces at the side seams, and sew the lower jacket to the upper jacket. The front pieces will extend beyond the upper jacket to create the facing.

4. Fold over the lower fronts even with the upper fronts to create front facings. Press.

Sew the lower jacket pieces to the upper jacket, aligning pieces at the side seams.

Sewing the Curved Seams
Refer to Chapter One.

1. Lay the jacket completely flat, wrong side facing up. Place the Curve C guide along the sleeve stitch line at the back, and draw a line along the curve, extending 5" into the lower jacket. Repeat for the opposite side of the back.

2. Right sides together, fold the jacket along this line.

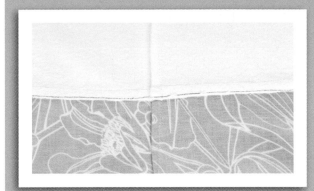

Mark the sewing line with pins.

3. Measure ¼" from the fold, and mark at the upper jacket seam line. Pin, narrowing to even with sleeve stitch line at upper end and 5" mark at opposite end. Sew along this line. Repeat for the opposite curve. The seam can also be made larger if needed by adding another ¼" to the measurement and still narrowing to the sleeve seam.

4. Press the curved seams toward the side seams.

Sewing the Side Seams
Refer to Chapter One.

Mark the side seam line.

1. Fold jacket along the underarm seam line, right sides together. At the seam line on the side seam, measure 1" in, and mark.

2. From this point, draw a line that gradually becomes ½" at either end of the seam.

3. Pin along this line, and try the jacket on before continuing.

4. If the jacket is too tight, add another ¼" to the measurement and redraw the line. If the jacket needs to be looser, reduce the line by ¼".

5. Sew seams and trim excess.

6. Press seams flat. Topstitch along either side of the seam lines.

7. Press under ½" along the lower edge of the jacket.

8. Press under 1½", hem, and apply iron-on tape. Topstitch.

Sewing the Front Trim Bindings

1. Press ½" under along each side of the two pieces of floral front trim. Press the top edges under ½" also. Fold the trim pieces in half, and press.

2. Press the pink trim pieces in half.

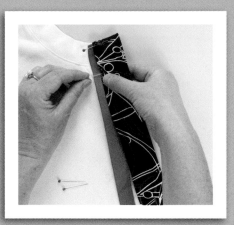

Step 3

3. Beginning at the top of the neckband, pin the front floral trim in place and insert the pink along the inside edge. Repeat for the opposite front. Cut off any excess at the bottom, leaving ½" to turn in even with the hem edge.

4. Topstitch along both the sides and ends of the front trim. Press.

COLLAR

1. Press interfacing to either side of the collar. Pin the interfaced collar pieces right sides together.

2. Sew seam all around, leaving a 2" opening to turn along the lower end.

3. Trim the corners and seam. Turn the collar, and press.

4. Topstitch the collar on three sides. Do not topstitch the lower end.

5. Pin the right side lower edge of the collar to the wrong side lower edge of the neckband, matching the center backs. The collar will not extend to the ends of the ribbing.

6. Sew along the bottom edge, using the topstitch line as a guide. Press seam.
7. Flip the collar to the right side of the jacket. Topstitch the lower edge.
8. Hand-stitch the ribbing to the collar lining to give the collar a finished look.

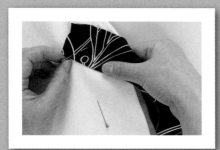

Step 9

9. Fold the front edges of the neck ribbing over to form a triangle. Pin.
10. Fold all lapel squares diagonally, right sides together.
11. Sew seams along three sides, leaving a small opening for turning. Turn and press.
12. Pin the floral triangle over the pink, with the end extending ½" under the front collar edge. Repeat for the opposite side.
13. Topstitch in place.

CUFFS

1. Press interfacing to half of the wrong side of the two floral cuff pieces.
2. Align the pink cuff pieces to the floral cuff pieces, right sides together.
3. Sew along both long sides, leaving a 2" opening to turn.

Step 4

4. Press the cuffs flat, with pink centered at the top.
5. Sew along the short ends. Clip corners.

6. Turn and press.
7. Press to right side ½" on end of sleeves.
8. Pin cuffs to the sleeve, extending more than 2" from the sleeve end. The cuff ends should meet at the underarm seam. Topstitch in place. Try the jacket on to check the sleeve length. Trim the sleeve if necessary. The cuff extends over the sleeve edge, so it can be adjusted to fit your arm length.

Adding Closures

1. Sew buttons 3½" apart, with the second button at the jacket front seam line.
2. Fold the trim into two loops.
3. Mark loop placement on the opposite side.
4. Sew loops to the inside front binding with small stitches. Take stitches through the back of the binding only.

ACCENT, ALTER AND ACCESSORIZE!

In general, the most flattering jacket styles play up your assets and hide your figure challenges.

— Diana

Accent

- Add matching fabric pink buttons to the front and to the cuffs.

- Embroider a similar floral design with pink or black thread on the upper jacket.

- Add a narrow pink trim edge to the bottom hem of the jacket.

Alter

- Change colors: Try chocolate brown and teal

- Shorten or lengthen for height. The jacket can be shortened to the hip line.

- For a fuller bust, lengthen the top of the jacket and use a darker color on top.

Accessorize!

- Boat-neck sweater

- Black trousers

- Leather pumps

- Pink messenger bag

- Silver hoops

TROPICAL TEAL

A bold print paired with black is a dynamic combination, and this bright jacket is sure to impress. A distinctive front closure completes this jacket with compelling contrasts. Learn to cut a sweatshirt at interesting angles to complete this project.

MATERIALS:

* 1 black sweatshirt
* ⅔ yd. black, white and teal floral fabric
* ⅔ yd. teal fabric
* ½ yd. interfacing
* 3" square of quilt batting
* 3 square 1" black buttons
* 2 square hook-and-loop closures
* Iron-on adhesive tape
* Matching thread
* Sewing notions listed in Chapter One

Finished Length: 27"

PATTERNS:
Collar, Cuff, Upper, Lower Front Facings and Curved C Guide pieces from the Pattern Sheet
"Tropical Teal" is #2 on the Pattern Sheet

33

CUTTING PLAN:

- ❇ Cut two upper-front facing pieces from floral fabric
- ❇ Cut two lower-front facing pieces from floral fabric
- ❇ Cut two upper-front facing pieces from teal fabric
- ❇ Cut two lower-front facing pieces from teal fabric
- ❇ Cut two cuff pieces from floral fabric
- ❇ Cut two cuff pieces from teal fabric
- ❇ Cut two cuff pieces from interfacing
- ❇ Cut one upper collar piece from floral fabric
- ❇ Cut one under collar piece from teal fabric
- ❇ Cut two collar pieces from interfacing
- ❇ Cut two 2½" front closure squares from teal fabric
- ❇ Cut one 2½" square from quilt batting

Black Sweatshirt

cut off neck

19"

cut along lines

cut off cuffs

cut off band

Tropical Teal
Jacket Length
Body Type: Apple
Black Sweatshirt: L
Embellished Closure
Angled Cuffs

Back of the jacket.

Reviewing Chapter One before you begin will be very helpful. Sew ½" seams with pieces right sides together unless otherwise indicated.

Cutting the Sweatshirt

1. Refer to the Inspiration Board for a cutting diagram for the sweatshirt. Cut off the band and cuffs.
2. Cut the sweatshirt open along the underarm seams, and cut off the neckband.
3. Lay the sweatshirt flat, wrong-sides up. Measure and draw the center front line.
4. Measure 10" up from the bottom on the center front line. Mark.

5. Use the front facing pattern pieces as a guide. Place them in position, overlapping at the 10" mark to create an angle. The measurement from the neck edge should be approximately 19" to the 10" mark.
6. Draw along these lines. Add ½" to the lines for the seam allowance, and redraw.
7. Cut along these front lines.
8. Press along the first ½" line, pressing to the front side of the sweatshirt. Press 1" hem along the jacket front.

 Step 8 is in preparation for adding front facings and does not require any sewing.

Step 5

Sewing the Curved Seams
Refer to Chapter One: Curved Seam

1. Lay the jacket completely flat, wrong side facing up. Place the Curve C guide along the back sleeve stitch line, and draw a line along the curve to the bottom edge. Repeat for the opposite side of the back.
2. Right sides together, fold along these lines.
3. Measure and mark ¼" in from this line at the lower edge. Pin at this point, narrowing into even with the sleeve stitch line.
4. Sew along this line. Repeat for opposite side. Press.

Sewing the Front Facings

1. Align all facings right sides together, pairing one floral with one teal piece.
2. Sew ¼" seams around each facing, leaving a 2" opening to turn.
3. Clip corners and curves. Turn right sides out. Press.
4. Leave the front hem folded, and pin the lower facings even with the folded edge. Pin in place. Topstitch around all four sides. Press.
5. Pin the upper facings in place, overlapping the lower facings. Topstitch in place on all four sides. Press.

Step 4

Collar

1. Press interfacing to either side of collar. Pin interfaced collar pieces right sides together.
2. Sew seam all around, leaving an opening to turn.
3. Trim corners and seam. Turn collar and press.
4. Topstitch collar on three sides. Do not stitch the lower edge.

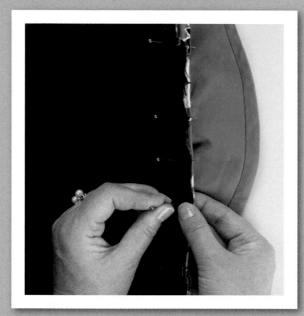

Pin the collar in place along the neck edge.

5. Pin the right side lower edge of collar to the wrong side lower edge of the neck, matching the center backs. The collar will extend over the ends of the upper facings.
6. Sew along the lower edge. Press seam.
7. Flip the collar to the right side of the jacket. Press.

Cuffs

1. Press interfacing to cuffs.
2. Align cuff pieces, pairing floral with teal.
3. Sew on all four sides, leaving a 2" opening along the bottom. Clip corners. Turn and press.
4. Topstitch cuffs on two diagonal sides.
5. Press ½" under on the ends of the sleeves. Topstitch in place.

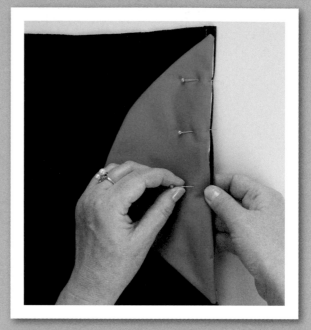

Step 6

6. Pin right sides of cuffs to wrong side of sleeve edges. Sew seam.
7. Fold cuff over to right side and press.
8. Sew buttons to cuff points through the sweatshirt.
9. Turn and press.
10. Press to right side ½" on sleeve ends.

When I designed this jacket, I sewed the cuffs to the raw sleeve edge. Adding a hem to the sleeve first will give it a more finished appearance.

Sewing the Side Seams
Refer to Chapter One.

1. Fold jacket right sides together along the underarm seam line. Mark the halfway point at the side seam, measure 1" in, and mark.
2. From this point, draw a line gradually becoming ½" at either end of the seam.
3. Pin along this line, and try the jacket on before continuing.
4. If the jacket is not fitted enough, add another ¼" to the measurement and redraw the line. If the jacket needs to be looser, reduce the line by ¼".

5. Sew seams. Finish and press.

6. Press a 1" hem along the remaining lower edge of the jacket.

7. Apply iron-on adhesive. Press.

8. Sew two rows of topstitching, beginning at the edge of the front facing.

Adding Closure

1. Align squares right sides together, with quilt batting on one wrong side.

2. Sew along all four sides with ¼" seam, leaving 1" opening.

3. Clip corners. Turn right-side out and press.

4. Sew the opening shut with small stitches.

5. Sew the button to the center of the square on the diagonal.

Step 6

6. Sew hook-and-loop squares to the front and back of the front facings where they overlap.

7. Sew loop square to the front of the over-lapped facing.

8. Sew hook square to the back of closure square, turning it to be a diamond.

Optional Lining

1. Cut a rectangle 12" by 25".

2. Using the top neck edge as a guide, cut a top curve in the lining piece.

3. Mark the center bottom. Measure 4" on either side of the center.

4. Place a ruler on the diagonal from these marks to the upper edge.

5. Draw and cut along this line.

6. Press ¼" under on all four sides.

7. Topstitch on all four sides. Press.

8. Center and pin the curved end along the collar edge.

9. Hand stitch in place.

10. Tack at the halfway point and lower edge.

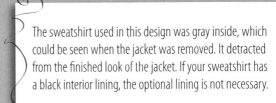

The sweatshirt used in this design was gray inside, which could be seen when the jacket was removed. It detracted from the finished look of the jacket. If your sweatshirt has a black interior lining, the optional lining is not necessary.

ACCENT, ALTER AND ACCESSORIZE!

Wearing all one color from head to toe draws the eye up and down and makes you look tall and thin. You can match the same color from head to toe, or opt for slight variations of the same color family. Light and bright colors will make you look bigger; dark and muted colors will make you look smaller.

– Diana

Accent

- Add seed beads to the facings.

- Embroider similar floral designs with teal thread on the jacket.

- Add piping to the edges.

Alter

- Change colors: Try chocolate brown and pink.

- For a fuller hip, omit the lower facings and let the jacket fall straight.

Accessorize!

- Teal shirt

- Black gauchos

- High boots

- Square tote

POLKA DOT PIZZAZZ

There is something about polka dots that is very appealing, and they make a bold fashion statement in black and white. I was inspired by this beautiful scarf, which led to a scissors-happy day with an abundance of black and white sweatshirts! I started cutting, and two sweatshirts became one unique wrap jacket with a flattering asymmetrical hemline.

MATERIALS:

* ❀ 1 black sweatshirt
* ❀ 1 white sweatshirt
* ❀ 1 pkg. double-fold black bias tape
* ❀ 2 yd. ¼" black trim
* ❀ 56"-long polka dot scarf
* ❀ 4 black crochet beads
* ❀ 1 black snap
* ❀ Iron-on adhesive tape
* ❀ Matching thread
* ❀ Sewing notions listed in Chapter One

Finished Length: 18"-23"

PATTERNS:
Curve C Guide piece from the Pattern Sheet
"Polka Dot Pizzazz" is #3 on the Pattern Sheet

white Sweatshirt

cut off neck

cut along front lines

2"

cut off 60° angle

cut off cuffs

cut off band

Polka Dot Pizzazz

Short Wrap

Body Type: Petite

2 S sweatshirts: B/W

Scarf Embellishment

Angled cuts

Black Sweatshirt

cut off neck

cut along front lines 2/3

2"

cut off cuffs

cut off 60° angle

cut off band

CUTTING PLAN:

❋ Cut 21" piece from the end of the scarf

Reviewing Chapter One before you begin will be very helpful. Sew ½" seams with pieces right sides together, unless otherwise indicated.

Cutting the Sweatshirts

1. Refer to the Inspiration Board for a cutting diagram for the sweatshirt. Remove the lower band, cuffs and neck from both sweatshirts.

2. Cut both sweatshirts open along the underarm seam lines.

3. Lay the white sweatshirt flat. Measure and cut 2" off both the front and back lower edges.

Back of the jacket.

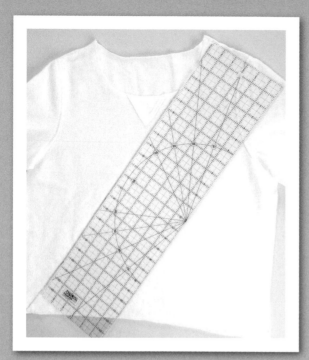

Step 4

4. Angle the ruler from the left shoulder seam to the bottom edge of the front. Draw a line, and cut along this line.

5. Measure the center back line, and cut down the center line. Set the smaller white half aside.

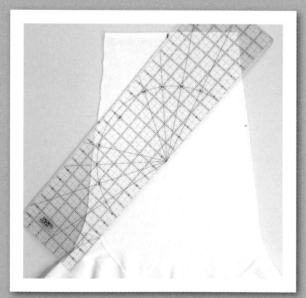

Step 6

6. Place left white pieces flat, wrong-side up. Mark the center point at both sleeve ends. With the ruler lined up square at the center point on the sleeve end, use the 60-degree angle to mark the

point farther up on the sleeve where the angle ends. Repeat for the opposite side of the sleeve. Cut along these lines.

7. Lay the black sweatshirt flat, wrong-side up. Measure and cut 2" off the back bottom edge.

8. Mark the center line, and cut along this line.

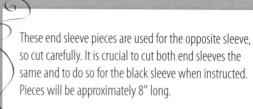

These end sleeve pieces are used for the opposite sleeve, so cut carefully. It is crucial to cut both end sleeves the same and to do so for the black sleeve when instructed. Pieces will be approximately 8" long.

9. Measure ⅔ of the way over on the sweatshirt front. Draw a straight line from neck to hem, and cut.

10. Set aside the smaller black half.

11. Measure 2" up from the bottom along the front underarm edge.

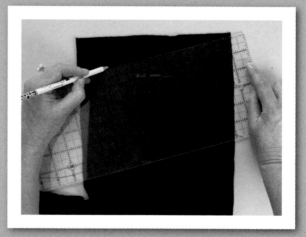

Step 12

12. Place the ruler on the diagonal from the front cut edge to this point. Draw and cut a line.

13. Repeat Step 6 with the black sweatshirt, and cut pieces off the end of the right sleeve.

Sewing the Sleeves

1. Align the black sleeve piece at the end of the white sleeve, right sides together. Pin and sew with a ¼" seam. Repeat for the opposite side. Finish and press.
2. Repeat for the opposite black sleeve with white pieces.
3. Topstitch with contrasting thread; white on black, black on white along inset pieces.
4. Fold and press the end of the sleeves under ½". Fold under again 1", and press.
5. Topstitch two rows with contrasting thread, ½" in for the first row and ¼" farther for the second row. Press.

Sewing the Curved Seams

1. Lay the jacket completely flat, wrong side facing up. Place the Curve C guide along the white back sleeve stitch line, and draw a line along the curve to the bottom edge. Repeat for the opposite side of the black back.
2. Right sides together, fold along these lines.
3. Measure and mark ¼" in from this line at the lower edge. Pin at this point, narrowing into even with the sleeve stitch line.
4. Sew along this line. Repeat for the opposite side. Press toward the side seams.
5. Topstitch with contrasting thread.

Sewing the Jacket

1. Align backs right sides together, and sew seam. Finish and press.

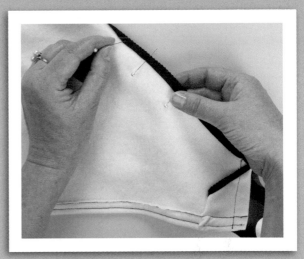

2. Begin applying bias tape at the black end point of the jacket front. Continue around the neck to the opposite end of the white front point. Topstitch in place. Press thoroughly.
3. Beginning at the same black point, pin black trim over bias tape. Stitch in place by hand or machine.

> The bias tape gives structure to the wrap front. The black trim gives a richer detail to the jacket, but it is an optional detail and can be omitted.

4. Measure 2" from the bottom of the black underarm front edge. Pin the raw end of the shorter scarf piece at this point. It should extend beyond the jacket.

Finishing the Jacket

1. Fold the jacket right sides together along the underarm seam line. At the halfway point on the side seam, measure 1" in and mark.

2. From this point, draw a line gradually becoming ½" wide at the end of the bottom and sleeve ends.

3. Pin along this line, and try the jacket on before continuing.

> If the jacket is too loose, add another ¼" to the measurement and redraw the line. If the jacket is too tight, reduce the line by ¼".

4. Sew seams and trim excess. Finish seams. Press. Turn right sides out.

5. Fold bottom hem under 1". Press. Use iron-on adhesive along the hem.

6. Topstitch two rows with contrasting thread.

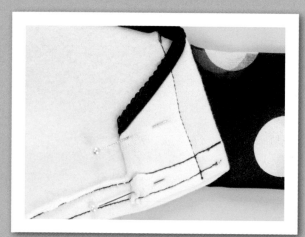

Step 7

7. Try on the jacket to determine the wrap overlap. Fold the white point under where it meets at the black side seam. Pin.

8. Fold the raw end of the longer scarf piece under ½". Pin to the shoulder seam ½" from the neck edge.

9. Topstitch the scarf in place.

10. Lay the scarf smooth along the diagonal line of the front, and topstitch the scarf where the lower edge is pinned.

11. Try the jacket on. Mark the placement of one snap (or two, if needed) along the diagonal edge.

12. Sew snap in place.

13. Sew two crochet buttons to the underside of each sleeve end, placing one on the seam line and the other 1½" apart.

ACCENT, ALTER AND ACCESSORIZE!

Create a focal point elsewhere on your body to draw attention away from your trouble spot. Examples: a fabulous hat, a large, eye-catching necklace or scarf, or a pair of knock-'em-dead shoes.

— Diana

Accent

- Bead the edge of the white front with black and white E beads.

- Machine embroider a circle design in contrasting thread on each section of the jacket.

Alter

- Change colors: Try white and navy with a red striped scarf.

- Create a jacket in right-sized sweatshirt for larger body types, adding length as needed.

- V-neck and three-quarter length sleeves visually elongate the body.

Accessorize!

- Lace cami

- Black trousers

- Leather pumps

- Clutch

- Pearl drop earrings

Often a fabric will inspire a design. I came across this unusual floral fabric with an Asian feel, and I thought the large flower pattern would be perfect for reverse appliqué. An embroidered linen piece was the perfect accompaniment; I added a raglan-sleeved sweatshirt, and soon a stunning jacket came to life. Be ready for many compliments when you wear this fashion-forward design.

MATERIALS:

* 1 black sweatshirt
* 1 yd. floral fabric
* ⅙ yd. embroidered linen fabric
* Black embroidery floss
* 1 decorative button
* 6 large black snaps
* Iron-on adhesive
* Basting glue stick
* Matching thread
* Sewing notions listed in Chapter One

Finished Length: 25"

PATTERNS:

Curve C Guide and Sleeve Gore pieces from the Pattern Sheet
"A Touch of the Orient" is #5 on the Pattern Sheet

CUTTING PLAN:

- ❀ Cut one 4" x 27" front strip from floral fabric

- ❀ Cut one 3" x 27" second front strip from floral fabric

- ❀ Cut one 5" x 27" front strip from embroidered linen

- ❀ Cut two sleeve gore pieces from floral fabric

- ❀ Cut three flowers from floral fabric

- ❀ Cut two 8" flower sections from floral fabric

- ❀ Cut one 6" flower section from floral fabric

* Refer to Sewing the Reverse Appliqués on pg. 46 before cutting.

Back of the jacket.

Reviewing Chapter One before you begin will be very helpful. Sew ½" seams with pieces right sides together, unless otherwise indicated.

Cutting the Sweatshirt

1. Refer to the Inspiration Board for a cutting diagram for the sweatshirt. Begin by removing the band and cuffs.

2. Cut open along underarm seam lines.

3. Lay the sweatshirt flat. Measure ⅔ over on the front of the sweatshirt, and draw a straight line with a ruler. Cut along this line.

Sewing the Left Front Trim Binding

1. Fold ¼" under on both long sides of the 3" floral strip.

2. Fold and press the strip in half, wrong sides together, to create band binding.

3. Fold one end of the strip in ½".

4. Beginning at the top of the neck ribbing, pin the band to the left side of the jacket, inserting the raw edge in between the binding. Trim off excess at bottom.

5. Topstitch binding in place.

Step 4

Sewing the Right Front Border

1. With three strands of black embroidery floss, backstitch to add more embroidery to the linen piece.

2. Align right sides together, and sew front 4" and 5" strips together on both long sides to create a long tube.

3. Turn the tube right-side out. Press with floral extending 1" beyond the linen to create a double border.

4. With the linen band facing in, measure 4½" down the floral outside edge and mark.

5. Angle a ruler from the mark to the top of the linen piece. Cut along this line.

6. Fold the cut end in ½" and press.

7. Topstitch along this end and down the floral inside front edge. Press.

8. Right sides together, pin the band to the raw edge of the right front. Sew this seam at ¼".

9. Trim excess off at bottom. Press.

10. Topstitch close to the seam line along the front edge of the jacket.

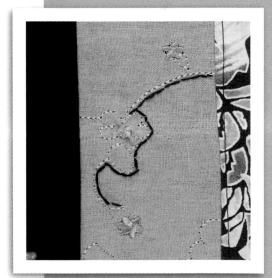

Embroider with backstitch.

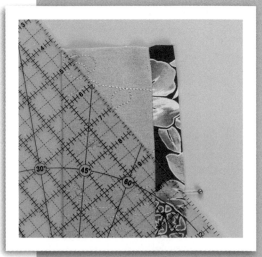

Mark the band to cut an angle.

Sewing the Reverse Appliqués

Step 1

1. Cut flowers from the fabric, allowing a ½" border around each cutout. For longer cutouts, cut floral sections from the fabric, allowing a ½" border around those also.
2. With a basting stick, apply appliqués wrong-side up to the wrong side of the jacket. Apply the stick just around the outside edge.
3. Apply three single flowers, ½" from the edge of the front band and spaced evenly on the front.
4. Apply 6" section, centered 1½" from the neck at the back.
5. Apply 8" sections, centered 1½" from the end of the sleeves.

For reverse appliqué, choose a shape that is easy to sew around and can be seen from the wrong side of the fabric.

Step 6

6. From the wrong side, sew around the flowers, following the outline of the pattern. Repeat for all floral sections. Trim threads.
7. From the right side, carefully cut your sweatshirt away from the flowers with sharp scissors. Begin by making a small slit in the center.
8. Cut close to the stitching on all floral sections. Press.

Sewing the Sleeves

Step 1

1. Align right sides together, and pin gore insert to one side of the sleeve, beginning with the end of the sleeve. Repeat for the other sleeve.

2. Sew this seam. Finish and press.

3. Press ½" under at sleeve ends. Repeat and press under again for hem.

4. Topstitch. Press.

Finishing the Jacket

1. Fold jacket right sides together along the underarm seam line. At the halfway point on the side seam, measure in 1" and mark.

2. From this point, draw a line gradually becoming ½" wide at the end of the bottom and sleeve ends.

3. Pin along this line, and try the jacket on before continuing.

> If the jacket is too loose, add another ¼" to the measurement and redraw the line. If the jacket is too tight, reduce the line by ¼".

4. Sew seams and trim excess. Finish seams. Press. Turn right sides out.

5. Lay the sweatshirt right-side up, overlapping the front band. Mark for placement of three snaps along the diagonal edge.

6. Press 1" hem along the lower edge of the jacket. Apply iron-on adhesive tape. Topstitch.

7. Mark the placement of three more snaps down the front.

8. Sew snaps in place.

Placement of snaps.

9. Sew a decorative button to the top of the neckband.

ACCENT, ALTER AND ACCESSORIZE!

Opt for a monochromatic look (all one color) to appear slimmer and taller.

— Diana

Accent

- Embroider the front band with more stitching.

- Add bead accents to the appliqués.

Alter

- Change colors: Try blue and natural.

- For a fuller bust, add more snaps.

- For fuller hips, make sure the bottom hem does not hit the widest part of the hips. Shorten or lengthen the jacket slightly.

- For a leaner look, choose a dark-colored sweatshirt.

Accessorize!

- White cami

- Tan linen pants

- Black flats

- Leather purse

- Drop earrings

CELEBRATION
OF CONTRASTS

The tunic is not exactly a jacket, but it's a very popular style. Easy to wear and an attractive style on everyone, this tunic is punched up with black accent trim. The triangle pattern in the fabric is repeated in the design with the flattering V-neck and prairie point detail on the three quarter sleeves. Subtle silver studs accent the fabric. Both comfortable and professional, this tunic is a great piece for the office.

MATERIALS:

- ❋ 1 white sweatshirt
- ❋ ½ yd. black and white geometric fabric
- ❋ 1 pkg. wide black bias tape
- ❋ 1 pkg. iron-on silver diamond nailheads
- ❋ 1 pkg. iron-on silver nailheads
- ❋ Heat-set crystal applicator
- ❋ Matching thread
- ❋ Sewing notions listed in Chapter One

Finished Length: 26"

PATTERNS:
Back Neck Facing and Front Insert pieces from the Pattern Sheet
"A Celebration of Contrasts" is #5 on the Pattern Sheet

white Sweatshirt

← cut off neck

10 1/4"

cut along dotted lines

cut off cuffs

cut off band

15"

celebration of contrasts

V neck Tunic

Body Type: Pear

White sweatshirt: M

Side Slits

Prairie Point Accent

CUTTING PLAN:

❀ Cut one front insert on the fold from fabric

❀ Cut one facing from fabric*

❀ Cut eight 4" squares from fabric

❀ Cut two bottom border pieces 12" x 20"

***Check the width of the sweatshirt before cutting.**

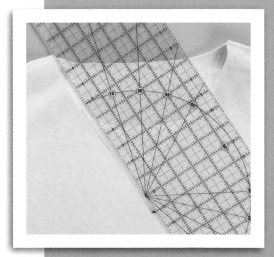

Back of the jacket.

Reviewing Chapter One before you begin will be very helpful. Sew ½" seams with pieces right sides together unless otherwise indicated.

Cutting the Sweatshirt

1. Refer to the Inspiration Board for a cutting diagram for the sweatshirt. Begin by removing the band, cuffs and neck.
2. Cut the sweatshirt open along the underarm seams.
3. Measure from the underarm seam down the arm 15", and draw a line. Cut both sleeves off at this line.
4. Lay the sweatshirt flat. Measure down from the neck center front 8".
5. Angle a ruler from this point to the shoulder seam. This should measure 10¼". Draw a line, and repeat for the opposite side. Cut along these lines.

Step 5

Finishing the V-neck

1. Fold and press the bias tape in half.

2. Finish the lower edge of the facing. Pin the upper edge of the facing to the back neck edge of the sweatshirt.

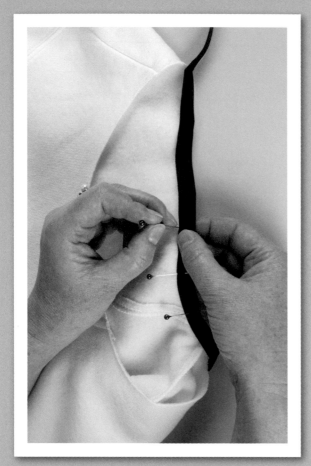

Step 3

3. Begin at the back, and pin bias tape over the raw neck edge. Pleat at the front V point. Overlap the ends ¼", and cut off excess at shoulder.

4. Fold the front insert in half. Press. Finish raw edges.

5. Pin the front insert into front V.

6. Topstitch along the bias tape, beginning at the back of the neck, catching the facing and front insert pieces with stitching.

Finishing the Sleeves

1. Pin and topstitch bias tape along both sleeve ends. Press.

2. Press squares into prairie points.

Step 3

3. Overlap four prairie points ½" along the inside edge of each sleeve. Topstitch in place.

4. Press and finish raw edges.

Finishing the Bottom Border

1. Measure the bottom front and back of the sweatshirt from seam to seam, and check against the border pieces width. Border pieces should match the measurement on each piece. Trim pieces if necessary.

2. Fold the border pieces in half, right sides together. Sew side seams. Trim. Finish seams.

3. Turn pieces right sides out. Press. Finish top edges.

4. Pin and sew bias tape along both lower edges, front and back.

Step 5

5. Pin the border pieces to the inside edge of the bottom bias tape, leaving ½" on either end for the seam.

6. Topstitch in place. Press.

Finishing the Tunic

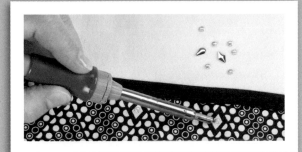

Step 1

1. Using the heat-set applicator, place nailheads according to manufacturer's instructions. Apply to repeating pattern elements on the front insert, prairie points, and front and back borders.
2. Fold the tunic right sides together along the underarm seam line. At the halfway point on the seam, measure 1" in and mark.
3. From this point, draw a line gradually becoming ½" wide at the end of the edges. Refer to Chapter One.
4. Pin along this line, and try the tunic on before continuing. If the tunic is too loose, add another ¼" to your measurement and redraw the line. If the jacket is too tight, reduce the line by ¼".
5. Sew seams and trim excess. Finish seams. Press. Turn right-sides out.

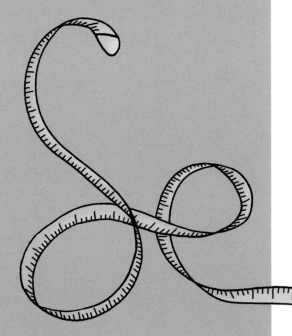

ACCENT, ALTER AND ACCESSORIZE!

If you opt for a comfortable, well-made piece in a style that flatters your figure and works well in your existing wardrobe, you'll be able to wear it for years to come.

— Diana

Accent

- Apply silver studs evenly along the bias tape.
- Add diamond-shaped fabric patches to the elbows.
- Accent a dropped waistline with a wide satin ribbon tied at the side.
- Alternate solid black prairie points with the pattern on the sleeves.

Alter

- Change colors: Try black and lavender.
- This tunic can work for all body types. Shorten or lengthen it as necessary for height.
- Create the tunic in a right-sized sweatshirt for larger body types.
- V-neck and three-quarter length sleeves visually elongate all body types.
- Choose reverse contrast for a fuller upper body; use a black sweatshirt with a similar border.

Accessorize!

- White cami
- Pencil skirt
- Pumps
- Boston bag
- Earrings

CHAPTER THREE

Jeans and tees are an easy and comfy choice for weekend wear. Throw on a great-looking vest or jacket, and you have an outfit for movies, shopping or lunch out with the girls. Grab one of these eye-catching toppers, and your friends will all want one (or try and get you to make one for them!). Plan a sewing get-together, and you will all be dressed in style.

GIRLS JUST WANT TO HAVE FUN

IN VESTED STYLE

Let's play in this striking quilted vest. Team it with jeans and a cozy sweater, and head out for a walk in the woods — or a walk on the wild side! Prairie-point detail is inspired by the colorful fabric choice, and the quilted stripes add extra warmth.

MATERIALS:

- ✳ 1 red sweatshirt
- ✳ 1 yd. main striped fabric
- ✳ 1 yd. coordinating fleece
- ✳ 2 fat quarters solids or batiks
- ✳ ⅓ yd. lightweight quilt batting
- ✳ ¼ yd. interfacing
- ✳ 2 buttons, 1½" diameter
- ✳ 3 large black snaps
- ✳ Matching thread
- ✳ Sewing notions listed in Chapter One

Finished Length: 26"

PATTERNS:
Collar, Pocket and Bottom pieces from the Pattern Sheet
"In Vested Style" is #6 on the Pattern Sheet

CUTTING PLAN:

- ❋ Cut four bottom pieces from striped fabric
- ❋ Cut four bottom lining pieces from fleece
- ❋ Cut one collar from striped fabric
- ❋ Cut one collar lining from discarded bottom of sweatshirt
- ❋ Cut one collar piece from interfacing
- ❋ Cut two pocket pieces from fleece or solid
- ❋ Cut two 4½" x 30" front band pieces from striped fabric
- ❋ Cut eight 4" x 4" squares of each solid
- ❋ Cut two 2" x 6½" pocket facings from solid

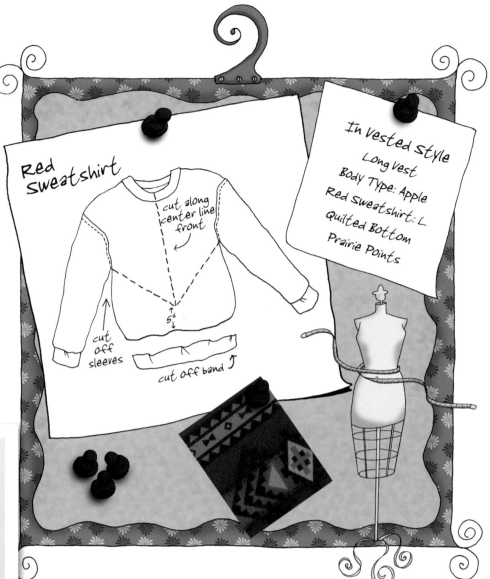

Red Sweatshirt

cut along center line front

cut off sleeves

cut off band ↑

In Vested Style
Long Vest
Body Type: Apple
Red Sweatshirt: L
Quilted Bottom
Prairie Points

Back of the vest.

Step 5

Reviewing Chapter One before you begin will be very helpful. Sew ½" seams with pieces right sides together unless otherwise indicated.

Cutting the Sweatshirt

1. Refer to the Inspiration Board for a cutting diagram for the sweatshirt. Begin by removing the band.

2. Cut open along the underarm seam lines.

3. Cut off sleeves 1" beyond the sleeve seam line.

4. Lay the sweatshirt flat. Mark the center front and back along the lower edge.

5. Measure up from the center mark 5". Line up the ruler on the diagonal from ¾" below the underarm seam to the center mark. Draw a line with the quilt pencil. Repeat for the second side of the sweatshirt and the back. Cut along these lines.

Sewing the Pocket Facings

1. Draw a center line on each facing, stopping ¾" from the ends.

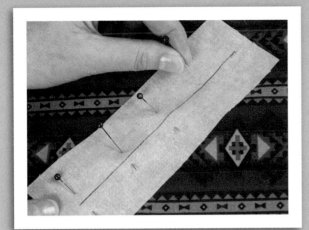

Step 2

2. Refer to the bottom pattern piece for placement of the pocket facings. Right sides together, pin the pocket facings in place on the striped fronts.

3. Using the center line as a guide, sew ¼" on all four sides of the line.

4. Clip along the solid center line and into the corners just to the stitching. Turn and press to the inside of the front. Repeat for the second pocket facing.

Sewing the Lower Jacket

1. Sew ¼" back seam of bottom pieces, right sides together. Press seam open.

2. Sew the front and back pieces right sides together at the side seams. Press seams open.

3. Repeat steps 1 and 2 for the bottom fleece lining. Trim seams before pressing.

4. Pin fleece and fabric pieces right sides together, aligning the seams. Sew, leaving the top open.

5. Clip corners and trim seam. Turn right-side out and press well.

6. Topstitch around the pocket openings.

Step 7

7. Carefully trim the lining in the pocket opening to the topstitching.

8. Machine or hand quilt the lower jacket along the stripes. Clip all threads and press.

9. Topstitch the bottom edge.

Inserting the Pockets

1. Sew the pocket pieces right sides together. Finish seam.

2. Turn the pocket right-side out. Press.

3. Press and sew ¼" hem on the top edges of the pocket.

4. Pin the pocket in place, lining the seams up at each end of the pocket opening. The pocket should angle toward the center front of the lining.

5. Hand-sew the pocket in place. Backstitch, going through the fleece lining only. Repeat for the second pocket.

Sewing the Armholes

1. Try on the upper vest to check for shoulder position. Place a pin at the top of the shoulder seam where the shoulder should be.

2. Turn wrong-side out, and use a ruler to draw a line from the underarm seam to the pinned shoulder mark. Fold and press along this line.

3. With fold flat, sew ¾"-long underarm seam.

4. Topstitch armholes at the 1" mark at the top of the shoulders, narrowing to ¼" at the under-arm. Trim off any excess fabric. Press.

Sewing the Vest Together

1. Pin the bottom section right sides together, lining up the underarm seams.

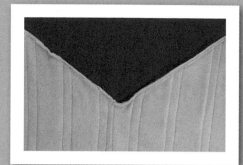

Inside center back seam.

2. Begin at the center back. Sew seam.
3. Press seam. Topstitch.

Sewing the Prairie Points

1. Press solid squares into prairie points.
2. Alternating colors, pin prairie points ½" from the center jacket line. Overlap the edge ¼" and sew in place.
3. Use a zigzag or alternate decorative stitch and coordinating thread to outline the points.

Adding the Front Trim

1. Press ½" under along each side of the two pieces of front trim. Press the top edges inside ½" also.
2. Fold the trim pieces in half wrong sides together and press.
3. Beginning at the top of the neckband, pin the front trim in place. Cut off excess at the bottom, leaving ½" to press inside.
4. Pin in place, covering the raw edges of the prairie points.
5. Topstitch along both sides and ends of the front trim. Press.

Sewing the Collar

1. Press interfacing to the wrong side of the collar.
2. Pin the collar pieces right sides together. Sew seam all around, leaving an opening to turn.
3. Trim the corners and seam. Turn the collar and press.

4. Topstitch the collar on three sides, but not on the lower edge.
5. Pin the right-side bottom edge of the collar to the wrong-side lower edge of the neckband.
6. Sew along the bottom edge, using the neckband topstitch line as a guide. Press seam.
7. Flip the collar to the right side of your jacket.
8. Hand-stitch ribbing to the collar lining to give the collar a finished look.

Finishing the Vest

1. Loosely hand-stitch the bottom corner of the pockets to the lining.
2. Decide on snap location (approximately 6", 8" and 10" from the neck). For a fuller bust, closures should come above and continue below the bust line. For a fuller hip, place closures slightly higher, or limit yourself to two. If desired, add buttons as a decorative embellishment.
3. Sew snaps in place on the front trim.
4. Sew buttons in place.

Accent, Alter and Accessorize!

The most flattering shapes for collars are the opposite of your face shape, since the shapes are so close to one other. A round collar would visually widen a round face, for example, while a long, angular collar would thin and elongate a round face. Small faces and necks call for small collars; large faces and necks call for large collars.

— Diana

Accent

- Quilt the collar.

- Add decorative stitches to the prairie points.

Alter

- Change colors: Try using black and white.

- For a leaner look, keep fabrics very close to the main vest color, and always use a vertical pattern.

Accessorize!

- Gold crewneck sweater

- Navy pants

- Black loafers

- Tote bag

OH SEW BLUE

Denim is a must-have in every wardrobe. I found lots of great jeans at a local thrift shop — but alas, they were all in sizes too small to wear! Some other finds included a jean jacket, which was too large, and a colorful knit sweater with gorgeous horizontal stripes (a definite no-no). The answer? Cut them up and put them all together with a washed denim sweatshirt to create a handsome three-quarter-length jacket.

MATERIALS:

* 1 denim-blue sweatshirt
* 3 pairs adult jeans
* 1 jean jacket
* 1 striped or patterned sweater, any size
* Scraps of green fleece
* 3 yd. each of four yarns in blues/burgundy
* 1 skein each of blue, burgundy, green and gold floss
* 2 metal buttons
* ⅓ yd. iron-on adhesive tape
* Fray check
* Matching thread
* Sewing notions listed in Chapter One
* 2" circle template

Finished Length: 36"

PATTERN:
Curved C Guide piece on the Pattern Sheet
"Oh Sew Blue" is #7 on the Pattern Sheet

CUTTING PLAN:

❋ Cut two 14½" x 25" front pieces from the jeans

❋ Cut one 26" x 25" back piece from the jeans

❋ Cut two 7" x 26" front trim pieces from the jeans

❋ Cut two back pockets from the jeans

❋ Cut two 6½" cuff pieces from the jean jacket

❋ Cut one front, collar, yoke and back continuous piece from the jean jacket

❋ Cut twelve 2" circles from the sweater

❋ Cut seven 1½" squares from the green fleece

Back of the jacket.

Reviewing Chapter One before you begin will be very helpful. Sew ½" seams with pieces right sides together unless otherwise indicated.

Cutting the Sweatshirt

1. Refer to the Inspiration Board for a cutting diagram for the sweatshirt. Cut off the band and cuffs.
2. Cut the sweatshirt open along the underarm seams.
3. Measure 6" down from the underarm seams. Cut the sweatshirt off along this line.
4. Cut open along the center front line.

Cutting Tips

Cut the legs off of the jeans.

Cut open the inside seams.

Press each piece flat. The hemmed ends of the legs will become the bottom of the jacket.

Sew the leg pieces right sides together to create your fabric. It is okay if the piece is larger, because it can be cut to size with the topstitched seam centered.

Cut around the back pockets, leaving 1" on all sides.

Cut along the front border of the jean jacket, leaving 1" on both sides and cutting close to the stitching around the lapels.

Cutting the Lower Jacket

1. Lay one jacket front piece flat, wrong-side up.
2. Measure in 3" at the top of the piece on one outside edge, and mark.
3. Line the ruler up from the bottom outside edge to mark at top.
4. Cut along this diagonal line for the side seam line.
5. Use this front piece as a pattern guide for cutting opposite front and back side seams.

Steps 2 and 3

Originally, I had planned to piece the lower jacket with several sections. I did this for the back of the jacket, but I didn't like how it looked. I decided to leave the back and create the front with longer leg pieces. With this jacket, you can piece the sections together as shown in the front and/or the back. Just make sure to look for long-legged jeans!

Yo-Yo Flowers, Leaves and Embroidery

1. Stitch around the outer edge of a knit circle with three strands of burgundy floss.
2. Pull the stitches tight. This will be the top of the flower. Leave the needle and floss attached.
3. Place the flower on the pocket. Take the floss from the center of the flower, across the flower through the pocket front only, and back through the center of the flower. Pull slightly to create a flower shape. Repeat for the opposite side of the flower.
4. Take the needle through the center of the flower again. Secure with a couple of small stitches, and cut threads.
5. To make the leaves, cut 1½" squares across the diagonal into triangles.
6. Gather the wide end of the triangle with green floss to create the leaf.
7. Backstitch along the lines of the pocket with three strands of burgundy.
8. Cross stitch along the pocket lines with three strands of green floss.
9. Repeat for the second pocket.

Embroidered pocket.

59

10. Cut open the seams of the denim cuffs. Trim ¼" off on either side of seam.
11. Sew flowers to the cuffs.
12. Backstitch with burgundy floss to embroider the vine between the flowers.
13. Attach leaves with green floss. Take the floss over the leaf with four small stitches to secure and shape.
14. Cross stitch six to eight stitches around each leaf with green floss.
15. Backstitch in burgundy along the front band of the jacket.

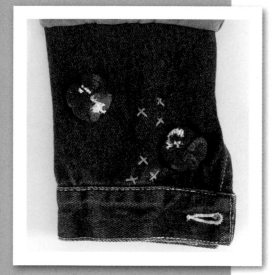

Embroidered cuff.

Sewing the Curved Seams

1. Lay the upper jacket completely flat, wrong side facing up. Place the Curve C guide along the sleeve stitch line, and draw a line along the curve. Repeat for the opposite side of the front and back.
2. Right sides together, fold along these lines.
3. Measure and mark ¼" in from this line at the lower end. Pin, narrowing to even with the sleeve stitch line at the upper end.
4. Sew along this line. Repeat for the opposite front and back. Press.
5. Topstitch.

Sewing the Upper Jacket

1. Cut 1" from the front band of the jean jacket, and carefully cut close to the topstitching along the yoke. Leaving the collar attached, continue around the back of the jacket. Repeat for the opposite side.
2. Apply fray check along this cut edge. Let dry.
3. Clip into the corners where the yoke and front band meet.
4. Right sides together, pin the band to the front edge with the top of the neckband even with the collar edge.
5. Cut any excess off of the end of the band.
6. Repeat for the opposite side of the band, making sure the buttons and buttonholes line up.
7. Continue pinning all the way around, stretching the neckband slightly to fit the collar if needed.
8. Sew the front band seam close to the edge up to the yoke. Finish and press.

Cutting the jean jacket front.

9. Topstitch the collar to the top of the neckband.

10. Hand-stitch the outer edge of the yoke to the sweatshirt.

11. Twist yarn together, and hand-stitch along the raw edge of the yoke. Trim off excess at opposite front.

12. Embroider the yoke. Refer to the yo-yo embroidery section for sewing flowers and leaves.

13. Backstitch with burgundy floss to embroider the vine between the flowers.

14. Attach leaves with green floss. Take the floss over the leaf with four small stitches to secure and shape.

15. Cross stitch six to eight stitches around each leaf with green floss.

16. Repeat for the opposite side and back of the yoke.

Sewing the Sleeves

1. Sew two rows of gathering stitches along the edge of each sleeve.

2. Pull the gathers to fit this edge.

3. Right sides together, pin the cuffs to the sleeve. Sew. Finish and press.

Sewing the Front Trim

1. Right sides together, pin the front trim pieces to the lower jacket front pieces, extending ½" beyond the bottom hem.

2. Fold the front trim in half and press, right sides together.

3. Sew ½" seam at the bottom of the trim to match the hem.

4. Clip corner. Trim and press.

5. Turn out to the right side of the jacket. Press.

6. Topstitch along either side of the trim.

Adding the Pockets

1. Carefully cut close to the topstitching along the pocket edges, leaving 1" at the top.

2. Apply fray check along the edges. Let dry.

3. Press the top under, even with the top of the pocket, and adhere with iron-on adhesive.

4. Measure down 5" from the upper edge of the jacket and 2" in from the front trim.

5. Place the top and side of the pocket at these marks. Sew in place along the topstitching.

Yoke embroidery.

Embroidered back of the jacket.

Sewing the Side Seams

1. Fold the upper jacket, right sides together, along the underarm seam line.

2. Sew seam.

3. Pin the front side seams to the back side seams of the lower jacket. Sew seams. Leave unfinished for the present.

4. Pin the lower front jacket to the upper jacket, matching side seams.

> If the upper jacket is larger than the lower jacket, sew gathering stitches along the upper jacket between the side seams and gather to fit the lower jacket.

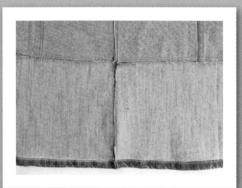

Inside view of jacket back.

5. Finish pinning the front upper and lower jacket together.

6. Sew seam. Finish and press.

7. Finish and press side seams.

Adding the Back Tab

1. Fold the back band piece in half, right sides together.

2. Sew seam, leaving a 2" opening.

3. Clip corners. Turn right-sides out, and press.

4. Topstitch all four sides.

5. Center the back tab at the center back between the upper and lower coat pieces.

6. Pull an extra 2" between the band ends. Pin.

7. Try on the coat to check how the back falls. Adjust fullness between band ends by adding or reducing the 2" measurement.

8. Sew the ends of the band in place.

9. Sew a button at both ends of the band.

ACCENT, ALTER AND ACCESSORIZE!

Three-quarter length jackets usually hit anywhere from mid-thigh to just above the knee. They are typically worn with pants, or with skirts or dresses that are the same length or a few inches longer than the jacket. Because of the amount of material involved, three-quarter length jackets tend to look best on women of average or tall height and those with long legs. The long vertical line created by the opening can be particularly slimming for tall, plus-size women.

— Diana

Accent

- Continue embroidering along the lower binding and hem.

- Add beads to the vine design and flower center.

Alter

- Change colors: try recycled corduroy pants in burgundy/red shades.

- Shorten or lengthen for height. The jacket can be shortened to the hip line.

- For a fuller bust, lengthen the top of the jacket.

Accessorize!

- White T-shirt
- Dark jeans
- Black boots
- Shoulder bag
- Silver hoops

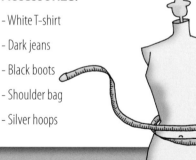

FRESH AND FEMININE

Finished Length: 18"

Very girly in dainty spring colors, this tweed-accented bolero is a perfect complement to jeans and a T-shirt. Add a little feminine touch to a comfy weekend outfit, and head out in style.

MATERIALS:

* 1 mauve sweatshirt
* 1 yd. tweed fabric (loose weave)
* 1 ball fashion yarn
* 1 package 1"-wide elastic
* 6" square leaf-green felt
* 1 pin back
* Matching thread
* Sewing notions listed in Chapter One

PATTERNS:
Curved Front Guide, Collar and Leaf pieces from the Pattern Sheet
"Fresh and Feminine" is #8 on the Pattern Sheet

✿ Cut one collar piece
   from tweed

✿ Cut two 5" x 16" cuffs
   from tweed

✿ Cut six 30" strands from yarn

✿ Cut six 2 yd. strands from yarn

✿ Cut two leaves from felt

Back of the jacket.

*Reviewing Chapter One before you begin will be very helpful. Sew ½"
seams with pieces right sides together unless otherwise indicated.*

Cutting the Sweatshirt

1. Refer to the Inspiration Board for a cutting diagram for the sweatshirt.
Begin by removing the band and cuffs. Set the band aside for the
front trim binding.

2. Measure the center fold of the sweatshirt, and cut up the front
center line.

3. Cut 3" off the end of the sleeves and lower edge of the sweatshirt.

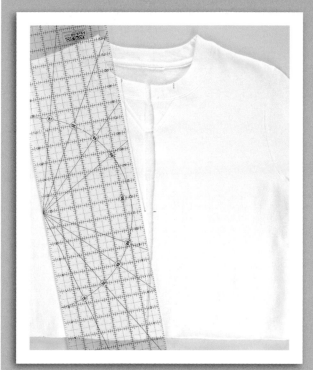

Step 4

4. Line up the front curve guide along the front edge of the sweatshirt. Draw a line and cut along this line for the front curve, cutting through the neck ribbing. Repeat for the other front edge of your sweatshirt. Stay stitch around all raw edges.
5. Try the jacket on at this point to determine length.

> Bolero-style jackets typically fall just above the natural waistline. When measuring for the hem, pin at the desired length, and then trim and hem any extra fabric.

6. Press raw edge under ½". Press 1½" hem, which will form the casing along the bottom.
7. Topstitch along the upper edge of the casing close to the edge. Topstitch ¼" in from this line again. Press.
8. Measure the elastic to fit comfortably, and add 1" to the measurement. Cut.
9. Use a safety pin attached to elastic to put through the casing. Pin the elastic at both ends of the casing.
10. Topstitch across both ends of the casing along the edge.

Sewing the Collar

1. Stay stitch 1½" in from the outside edges of the fringe on the collar and cuffs.

Step 2

2. Begin pulling threads from the outer edge of the collar and cuffs to create the fringe. Continue pulling until there is approximately 1" of fringe along the edge. It will be slightly uneven.
3. Trim fringe evenly.
4. Begin by matching the center back of the neck to the center seam of the collar, wrong sides together.

Step 5

5. Pin the edges together, pleating the collar with ½" pleats every 2" along one front side. Repeat for the opposite front side.
6. Begin at the center neck and stitch ¼" in from the edge. Remove pins. Press.

Adding the Band

1. Cut the bottom band ribbing in half lengthwise.
2. Right sides together, sew the short ends to make one long piece. Press seam.
3. Press ¼" under along one side.

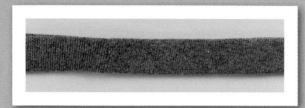

Step 4

4. Begin at the center back of the neck, aligning the seamed band to the neck edge, right sides together. Match the edges and pin over the top of the collar.
5. Continue pinning front to bottom, leaving ½" extending beyond the casing.
6. Trim off any excess on either end.
7. Sew along this edge from the end of one front to the other.
8. Flip the band to the inside.
9. Fold ½" excess at either end under and press.

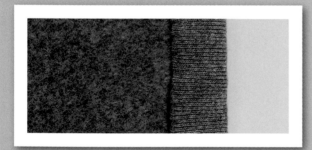

Step 10

10. Hand-stitch along this edge with small stitches.

Making the Cuffs

1. Fold the fringed cuff pieces in half, right sides together. Sew seam. Trim and press.
2. Slide the cuff over the end of the sleeve, matching edges. Pin in place, making small ¼" pleats every 1½".

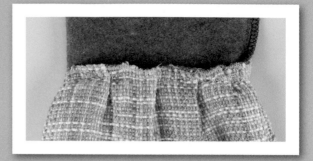

Step 3

3. Stitch around this seam. Trim and finish seam. Press.
4. Braid three 14" pieces together. Pin along the outer cuff and sleeve seam.
5. Start at the underarm seam, and sew in place with small stitches. Trim off any excess. Repeat for the second cuff.

Adding the Ties

1. Knot two sets of three 30" strands together for ties.
2. Pin a knot to the bottom of the front jacket trim, and hand-stitch in place. Repeat for the opposite front side.

Making the Flower Pin

Steps 1 and 2

1. Overlap the ends of the felt leaves. Hand-stitch together.
2. Take three 2 yd. strands of yarn and loop back and forth, creating loops approximately 4" long. Repeat for the second group of three strands.
3. Place both side by side, and tie thread tightly around the center.
4. Stitch the center of the loops to the over-lapped center of the leaves.
5. Sew the pin back to the center back of leaves.

ACCENT, ALTER AND ACCESSORIZE!

There are lots of ways to visually elongate (or unknowingly shorten) your body with clothes. You don't have to be a model size or height to look it; you just have to know what you have to work with and dress it appropriately. A few sleight-of-hand tricks are all it takes to look runway chic. Try it and see.

— Diana

Accent

- Exchange yarn trim for satin ribbon in three different widths.

- Add a large ribbon rose brooch.

- Add pearl trim to the sleeves along the front binding.

- Create a simple brooch by winding pearls into a circle and gluing them to a backing.

Alter

- Omit the elastic in the casing and wear with a monochromatic long silk shirt and pants.

- Add curved seams in the back for a slimmer look.

- Lengthen the jacket to your waist.

- Make the jacket in white-edged black with a black ruffled silk collar and satin ties.

Accessorize!

- Yellow cami

- Jeans

- Pearl studs

- White sandals

ATTITUDE PLUS

Regal red and royal purple have become a popular color combination for many women around the world. Living life to the fullest means having lots of time for fun, friends and laughter. This A-line jacket accented with ribbon appliqué and custom buttons is ready for the next fun event, no matter how outrageous! Flaunt your favorite colors with style!

MATERIALS:

* ❀ 1 red sweatshirt
* ❀ 1 yd. main floral fabric A
* ❀ 1 yd. coordinating flannel
* ❀ ⅛ yd. coordinating floral fabric B
* ❀ ⅛ yd. contrasting print fabric C
* ❀ ¼ yd. lightweight quilt batting
* ❀ 3 yd. 1"-wide purple ribbon
* ❀ 8 yd. ¼"-wide purple ribbon
* ❀ 1, 2 or 3 white 1½" buttons
* ❀ 2 white 1" buttons
* ❀ 3 large black snaps
* ❀ Decoupage medium
* ❀ Small brush
* ❀ Matching thread
* ❀ Sewing notions listed in Chapter One

Finished Length: 26"

PATTERNS:
Collar and Bottom pieces from the Pattern Sheet
"Attitude Plus" is #9 on the Pattern Sheet

Red Sweatshirt

cut along
center line
front

5"

cut off
cuffs

cut off band ↑

Attitude Plus

A-Line Jacket
Body Type: Apple
Red Sweatshirt: L
Ribbon Appliqué
Quilted collar/cuffs

CUTTING PLAN:

❋ Cut six 3" x 6" pieces from fabric B for collar

❋ Cut four bottom pieces from fabric A

❋ Cut four bottom lining pieces from flannel

❋ Cut one upper collar from fabric C

❋ Cut one under collar from fabric B

❋ Cut one collar from quilt batting

❋ Cut two cuffs 4½" x 14" from fabric B

❋ Cut two cuff linings 4½" x 14" from flannel

❋ Cut four 3" x 5" pieces from fabric C for cuffs

❋ Cut eight 3" x 5" pieces from fabric A for cuffs

Reviewing Chapter One before you begin will be very helpful. Sew ½" seams with pieces right sides together unless otherwise indicated.

Cutting the Sweatshirt

1. Refer to the Inspiration Board for a cutting diagram for the sweatshirt. Begin by removing the band.

2. Cut the sweatshirt open along the underarm seam lines.

3. Lay the sweatshirt flat. Mark the center front and back along the lower edge.

4. Measure 5" up from the center mark. Place the ruler on the diagonal, from ¾" below the underarm seam to the center mark. Draw a line with the quilt pencil. Repeat for the second side of the sweatshirt and back. Cut along these lines.

Back of the jacket.

Sewing the Lower Jacket

1. Right sides together, sew ¼" back seam of bottom pieces. Press seam open.
2. Sew the front and back pieces right sides together at the side seams. Press the seams open.
3. Repeat steps 1 and 2 for the fleece lining. Trim seams before pressing.
4. Pin fleece and fabric pieces right sides together, aligning seams. Sew, leaving the top open.
5. Clip the corners and trim the seam. Turn right-side out, and press well.
6. Topstitch the bottom edge.

Inside center back seam.

Sewing the Jacket Together

1. Align the upper-jacket underarm seams, and sew.
2. Pin the bottom section right sides together, lining up the underarm seams to the upper jacket.
3. Begin at the center back. Sew the seam.
4. Press seam.

Adding the Front Ribbon Trim

1. Beginning at the front edge of the jacket, topstitch ¼" ribbon along the seam line, continuing to the opposite front edge. Cut the ribbon and press.
2. Carefully measure from the top of the ribbing at the neck to the bottom edge of the jacket. Add 1" to the measurement, and cut four lengths of 1" purple ribbon.
3. Press the ends of the 1"-wide ribbon under ½". Starting at the top of the ribbing, pin to the front edge, extending ½" beyond the jacket edge.
4. Topstitch the ribbon to the front. Repeat for the opposite front side. Press.
5. Pin the two remaining pieces of ribbon to the inside edges of the ⅛" inside front ribbon.
6. Topstitch in place. Press.

Sewing the Collar

1. Pin the upper collar to the quilt batting.
2. Begin at the center collar back. Place the collar cut strips at slight angles spaced evenly on the right side of the upper collar. Stitch in place.
3. Place ¼"-wide ribbon strips over the stitch lines. Topstitch in place. Trim even with the collar.
4. Pin the collar pieces right sides together. Sew seam all around, leaving an opening to turn.
5. Trim the corners and seam. Turn collar and press.
6. Topstitch the collar on three sides, leaving the lower edge. Press.
7. Pin the right side bottom edge of the collar to the wrong side lower edge of the neckband.
8. Sew along the bottom edge, using the neckband topstitch line as a guide. Press seam.
9. Flip the collar to the right side of the jacket.
10. Hand-stitch ribbing to the underside of the collar for a polished look.

Steps 2 and 3

For more variety, hand-quilt flowers or other details in the fabric design and add small beads along the flower stems. A little extra sparkle is always a good thing!

Sewing the Cuffs

1. Begin at the center of the cuff strips. Place the strips at slight angles spaced evenly on the right side of the cuffs, as you did for the collar. Stitch in place.
2. Place ¼"-wide ribbon strips covering the stitch lines. Topstitch in place. Trim even with the cuff.
3. Align the cuff and cuff lining, right sides together. Sew around with ¼" seam, leaving a 2" opening. Repeat for the second cuff.
4. Clip corners. Trim seams slightly.
5. Turn right-side out. Press.
6. Try the jacket on to check sleeve length.
7. Fold the cuff in half, with the finished ends even. Sew a smaller button to the center of the end of the cuff. Repeat for the second cuff.
8. Slide a cuff onto the sleeve, lining up the end of the cuff with the underarm seam.
9. Hand-stitch in place near the top edge using a small running stitch. Go through the lining fabric only. Sew another row for extra strength. Repeat for the other cuff.

Adding a separate cuff makes adjusting the sleeve length a breeze. Trim sleeve ends if they are too long, or apply cuffs extending beyond the sleeve end for more length. You can also add a removable cuff with hook-and-loop tape or snaps.

Finishing the Jacket

1. Sew snaps to the ribbon front trim. Decide on placement. When adding closures, decide on placement with a couple of guidelines. For a fuller bust, closures should come above and continue below the bust line. For a fuller hip, closures can be slightly higher or limited to two. Buttons added as a decorative embellishment can number more or less than the actual closures.
2. Choose a design from your fabric scraps that will fit on the larger buttons. Three different elements were chosen for this jacket.

Steps 3, 4

3. Use button as a pattern guide and draw around the element. Cut out.
4. Paint a layer of decoupage medium on the button. Add a fabric circle.
5. Smooth over the top with another layer of decoupage medium.
6. Set aside to dry. Repeat for the other two buttons.
7. When dry, add another layer of decoupage medium.
8. When thoroughly dry, sew in place on the front ribbon trim of the jacket.

ACCENT, ALTER AND ACCESSORIZE!

It just goes to show that knowing yourself and having confidence in your assets is alluring at any age. You don't have to have a perfect figure to draw attention to the things you like about yourself. Simply emphasize what you like, and camouflage what you don't.

— Diana

Accent

- Quilt both collar and cuffs further.
- Add beads for a little sparkle.

Alter

- Change color: Try using purple with red accents.
- Lengthen the bottom to create a three-quarter length jacket, extending the A line seaming.
- For a leaner look, keep the bottom fabric very close to the main jacket color.

Accessorize!

- Purple T-shirt
- Black pants
- Red flats
- Shopper bag
- Hat

FOR THE ANIMAL IN YOU!

Every wardrobe needs a touch of animal print, and there are many beautiful synthetic furs and fabrics available. I found this gorgeous velvet in my favorite local fabric store. Ultra-soft and lightweight, the luxurious velvet complements this striking vest design. Create unique closures and a fringed collar for a one-of-a-kind versatile vest.

MATERIALS:

* 1 black sweatshirt
* ½ yd. animal-print velvet, fleece or fur
* 1 skein fashion yarn
* 4 black pompoms, ½" in diameter
* 2 matching 1" buttons
* 6"-wide piece of cardboard
* Waxed paper
* Iron-on adhesive tape
* Matching thread
* Sewing notions listed in Chapter One

Finished Length: 25"

PATTERNS:

Back Band and Curve Guide pieces from the Pattern Sheet
"For the Animal in You!" is #10 on the Pattern Sheet

CUTTING PLAN:

✻ Cut two 8" pocket squares from velvet

✻ Cut two 8" lapel squares from velvet

✻ Cut two 2" x 16" front trim pieces from velvet

✻ Cut one ½" x 18" collar fringe piece from velvet

✻ Cut two back tab pieces on fold from velvet

Back of the vest.

Step 5

Black Sweatshirt

cut along center line front

cut off sleeves

cut off band ↑

For the Animal in You
vest
Body Type: Petite
Black Sweatshirt: S
V Pockets
Yarn Accents

Reviewing Chapter One before you begin will be very helpful.

Cutting the Sweatshirt

1. Refer to the Inspiration Board for a cutting diagram for the sweatshirt. Begin by removing the band.
2. Cut open along the underarm seam lines.
3. Cut off sleeves 1" beyond the sleeve seam line.
4. Lay the sweatshirt flat. Mark the center front line and cut.
5. Fold the corner of the neck band over 2½", creating a triangle measuring approximately 6" long. Press and cut off the triangle. Repeat for the opposite front.

Sewing the Curved Seams

1. Lay the vest completely flat, wrong-side facing up. Place Curve C guide along the back sleeve stitch line, and draw a line along the curve. Repeat for the opposite side of the back.
2. Right sides together, fold along these lines.
3. Measure and mark ¼" in from this line at the lower end. Pin, narrowing to even with the sleeve stitch line at the upper end.
4. Sew along this line. Repeat for the opposite side of the back. Press.
5. Topstitch.

Sewing the Front Trim and Hem

1. Press under ¼" on all sides of the front trim pieces. Press in half.
2. Pin ½" up from the bottom along the straight edge of both sides of the vest fronts, allowing for the hem. Trim off any extra.
3. Topstitch the trim in place. Press from the wrong side with a pressing cloth.
4. Press ½" hem along the fronts and back.
5. Press 1" along the side seams to create slits at the side when the seam is sewn.
6. Apply iron-on adhesive tape.
7. Topstitch the sides, and hem the fronts and back.

Sewing the Lapels and Pockets

1. Fold the squares in half on the diagonal, right sides together with the nap running up and down.
2. Sew along both sides, leaving a 2" opening on all four pieces.
3. Clip the corners. Turn and press.
4. Pin two triangles with the nap running down to the top front of the vest. Topstitch in place.
5. Topstitch the long diagonal side of the remaining two triangles for pockets.
6. Pin the triangle pockets along the lower front edge of the vest.
7. Topstitch the pockets in place.
8. Press the arm openings under ½" and topstitch.

Sewing the Side Seams

1. Fold the vest right sides together along the underarm seam line. At the halfway point on the seam, measure 1" and mark.
2. Draw a line from this point, gradually becoming ½" at either end of the seam.
3. Pin along this line and try the vest on before continuing.

> If the vest is too loose, add another ¼" to your measurement and redraw the line. If the vest is too tight, reduce the line by ¼".

4. Sew seams to the slit and trim excess. Finish seams. Press.

Adding the Back Tab

1. Align the tab pieces right sides together.
2. Sew ¼" seam on all sides, leaving a 2" opening.
3. Clip corners. Turn right-side out and press.
4. Topstitch all four sides.
5. Center the back tab at the center back.

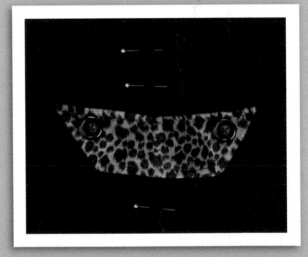

Step 6

6. Pull in the extra 1" between the band ends. Pin.
7. Try on the vest to check how the back falls. Adjust the fullness between band ends by adding or reducing the 2" measurement.
8. Sew the ends of the band in place.
9. Sew the buttons at each end of the band.

Making the Fringed Collar

1. Wind yarn around the cardboard with strands very close together.

Step 2

2. Slide the yarn off carefully, and center it on a thin 18" strip of velvet. Place a piece of waxed paper underneath the yarn as you sew, and then tear it away when you are finished.

3. Sew down the center of the yarn on the strip of velvet, pushing the strands together tightly as you sew.

4. Wind more yarn around the cardboard as needed to finish the neck strip. Repeat step 3.

5. Pin the yarn collar to the ribbing neck edge and hand-sew in place. Trim off any excess. I did not cut through the loops because I liked the look, but if you are not quite so loopy, cut through the ends of the strands for a fringed look.

> This adaptation of a popular front closure, the frog, is easy to make with pompoms and yarn. And you never know — it might turn into a prince!

Making the Front Frog Closures

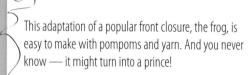

1. Cut two 36" pieces of yarn, and wrap each tightly around a pompom to create a ball. Continue wrapping until the pompom is completely covered and 1" in size, leaving 16" tails for loops. Cover the other two pompoms with 20" pieces of yarn.

Step 2

2. Hand-stitch through the four pompoms to keep the yarn in place.

3. Pin the pompoms to the front, 3" down from the lapel and 2" apart, centered just off the edge of the front trim. Try the vest on to determine the length of the loops.

4. Bring the end of the yarn tail to the pompoms, and knot. Sew all pompoms securely to the front of the vest.

ACCENT, ALTER AND ACCESSORIZE!

The shape of a bag should be the OPPOSITE of your own shape so as not to further emphasize it. If you're tall or thin, opt for a bag with curves; if you're curvy, opt for a bag with straighter lines. Otherwise, the shape of the bag will emphasize and exaggerate your own shape.

– Diana

Accent

- Add extra fringe around the armholes.

- Add longer fringe along the bottom.

Alter

- Change color: Try blue with denim trim.

- Create a vest larger body types and lengthen.

- For a fuller bust, add a third frog closure.

Accessorize!

- Camel sweater

- Chocolate pants

- Leather boots

- Suede satchel

PETITE PLAY

Buttercup yellow and ocean blue are a classic color combination. I had some beautiful fat quarters on hand with just the right shades of blue and yellow to complement the sweatshirt, and the dainty prints were perfect for creating a bolero-style jacket to fit a petite figure. Dressed up with a skirt for the office or as a topper for jeans and a T-shirt on the weekend, this versatile piece will be a favorite in your closet for years!

MATERIALS:

* 1 yellow sweatshirt
* 1 fat quarter floral fabric A
* 1 fat quarter floral fabric B
* 1 fat quarter striped fabric C
* 1 pkg. each 4mm E bead in blue, teal and yellow
* 10 green bugle beads, ½"
* 6 blue oval beads, 6mm x 8mm
* 4 green oval beads, 6mm x 8mm
* Iron-on adhesive tape
* Matching thread
* Sewing notions listed in Chapter One

Finished Length: 18"

PATTERNS:
Curve C Guide, Front Curve Guide and Bottom Curve Guide pieces from the Pattern Sheet
"Petite Play" is #11 on the Pattern Sheet

CUTTING PLAN:

✻ Cut eleven 4" prairie point squares from fabric A

✻ Cut eleven 4" prairie point squares from fabric B

✻ Cut eleven 4" prairie point squares from fabric C

Yellow Sweatshirt

cut along center line front

cut along ↓ line

cut off sleeves

3"

cut off band ↑

Petite Play

Bolero

Body Type: Petite

Yellow Sweatshirt: S

Prairie Points

Beaded Accents

Back of the jacket.

Step 6

Reviewing Chapter One before you begin will be very helpful. Sew ½" seams with pieces right sides together unless otherwise indicated.

Cutting the Sweatshirt

1. Refer to the Inspiration Board for a cutting diagram for the sweatshirt. Begin by removing the bottom band.

2. Cut open along the underarm seam lines.

3. Measure and cut up the front center line.

4. Lay the sweatshirt flat. Measure 10" down from the sleeve seam line. Cut the rest of the sleeve off at this point.

5. Measure and cut 3" off the bottom of the sweatshirt.

6. Line up the Front Curve Guide (found on the edge of the Sleeve Flounce) along the front edge of your sweatshirt. Draw a line, and cut along this line for the front curve. Repeat for the other front edge of the sweatshirt.

Sewing the Curved Seams

1. Lay your jacket completely flat, wrong side facing up. Place the Curve C guide along the front sleeve stitch line, and draw a line along the curve. Repeat for the opposite side of the fronts and back.
2. Right sides together, fold along these lines.
3. Measure and mark ¼" in from this line at the lower end. Pin, narrowing to even with the sleeve stitch line at the upper end.
4. Sew along this line. Repeat for the opposite side of the front and back. Press.
5. Topstitch.

Bolero-style jackets typically fall just above the natural waistline. When measuring for the hem, pin at the desired length, and then trim and hem any extra material.

Sewing Prairie Points

1. Press a ½" hem along the fronts, back and sleeve ends.
2. Press all squares into prairie points.
3. Pin the prairie points to the front inside edge of your jacket, beginning at the top of the ribbed collar.
4. Overlap the prairie points ½", alternating ABC points. The prairie points should end just before the end of the front jacket piece.
5. Topstitch in place ¼" from the edge. Repeat a second row of topstitch ¼" beyond the first row. Press.
6. Pin prairie points along the inside of the bottom edge of the sleeve, overlapping ½". Repeat for the second sleeve.
7. Topstitch in place ¼" from the edge. Repeat a second row of topstitching ¼" beyond the first row. Press.

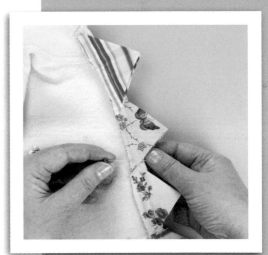

Step 4

Sewing the Side Seams

1. Fold the jacket right sides together along the underarm seam line. At the halfway point on the seam, measure 1" and mark.
2. From this point, draw a line gradually becoming ½" at either end of the seam.
3. Pin along this line and try the jacket on before continuing.
4. Sew seams. Finish seams. Press.
5. Hem the back of the jacket with topstitching, matching the front lines.

If the jacket is too loose, add another ¼" to the measurement and redraw the line. If jacket is too tight, reduce the line by ¼".

Beading the Jacket

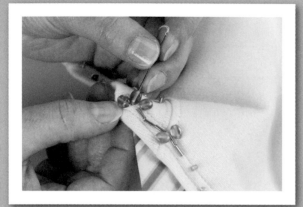

Step 1

1. Thread a fine needle with yellow thread. Begin at the ribbed collar. Anchor the thread at the back, and bring it through the front. Slide on a blue bead and return the thread to the back. Repeat in a curve with three blue beads to create a flower.

2. Slide on five bugle beads and take the needle to the back. Bring the needle to the front between the bugle beads to anchor them in place. Add a green bead on either side of the second bugle bead.

3. Add E beads approximately 1" apart along the topstitched lines of the front, back and sleeves. Repeat with an alternating row of beads.

Close-up of beading detail.

ACCENT, ALTER AND ACCESSORIZE!

So what, exactly, is a personal uniform? It's a collection of basic pieces that fit you well, highlight your assets, and make you feel great whenever you wear them — whether you had an hour to dress or five minutes to get out the door. These are the clothes and accessories that work in harmony with your body to make you feel taller, slimmer, bustier, hippier, or whatever, and that consistently bring you compliments. Once you've established what those elements are for you, work current versions into your wardrobe each season so that your look is always evolving yet consistent.

— Diana

Accent

- For extra detail, create a beaded flower design randomly all over the jacket.

- Extend prairie points around the back as well as the front.

Alter

- Change colors: Try spring green and soft pink.

- Lengthen the bolero to hit just below the waist to conceal a thicker middle.

- Make the bolero in a darker color without prairie points and with more beading near the face for a slimmer version.

Accessorize!

- Blue cami

- Dark jeans

- Espadrilles

- Canvas purse

CHAPTER FOUR

Living on the east coast with the changing seasons gives me lots of opportunities to wear jackets. Cool summer evenings, crunchy fall days and snowy winters all require warm outerwear. Throw in several holidays and special events throughout the cooler months, and the striking designs in this chapter will carry you easily through the holiday seasons. These jackets are not only wonderful to sew for yourself, but they are also perfect for gift giving.

'TIS THE SEASON

FALL FIESTA

Inspired by the swirling auburn and gold leaves, this cozy sweater-styled jacket is detailed with appliqué and beaded leaves. There are unlimited fabrics in the many vibrant hues and shades of fall. Use scraps or colorful fat quarters from your fabric stash to make this rich autumn jacket.

MATERIALS:

* ❋ 1 rust or orange sweatshirt
* ❋ ½ yd. brown plaid fabric A
* ❋ 1 fat quarter green check fabric B
* ❋ 1 fat quarter rust-print fabric C
* ❋ 1 fat quarter gold-print fabric D
* ❋ 26" brown jacket zipper
* ❋ Brown floss
* ❋ 1 package ½" orange bugle beads
* ❋ ¼ yd. iron-on adhesive
* ❋ Iron-on adhesive tape
* ❋ Matching thread
* ❋ Sewing notions listed in Chapter One

Finished Length: 29"

PATTERNS:
Curve Guide and Leaf pieces from the Pattern Sheet
"Fall Fiesta" is #12 on the Pattern Sheet

Rust
Sweatshirt

cut along
center
front
line

cut
off
cuffs

cut off band ↑

Fall Fiesta
Zipper Cardigan
Body Type: Apple
Rust Sweatshirt: L
Appliqué
Beaded

CUTTING PLAN:

❋ Cut two 8" pocket squares from fabric A

❋ Cut two 3" x 30" front trim strips from fabric A

❋ Cut four leaves from fabric B*

❋ Cut four leaves from fabric C*

❋ Cut four leaves from fabric D*

Apply adhesive to the fabric first.

*Reviewing Chapter One before you begin will be very helpful. Sew ½"
seams with pieces right sides together unless otherwise indicated.*

Cutting the Sweatshirt

1. Refer to the Inspiration Board for a cutting diagram for the sweatshirt. Begin by removing the bottom band and cuffs.
2. Cut open along the underarm seam lines.
3. Measure and cut up the front center line.

Finishing the Sleeves

1. Press the ends of the sleeves under ¼".
2. Press the ends of the sleeves under 1½" for the hem.
3. Topstitch two rows at 1" and 1¼" from the sleeve ends. Press.

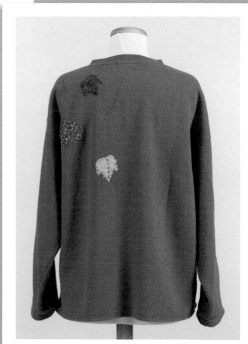

Back of the jacket.

Sewing the Pocket

1. Align the pocket squares right sides together. Sew around, leaving a 2" opening.
2. Turn the pocket right-side out. Press.
3. Fold the top of the pocket down 1" and press.
4. Fuse the rust leaf to the pocket.
5. Outline stitch around the leaf with two strands of floss.
6. Sew seven bugle beads to the center of the floss line, spaced slightly apart.
7. Pin the pocket to the front of the jacket 2½" from the bottom and front edge. Topstitch in place.

Applying the Leaves

Embroidered left front of jacket.

Embroidered right front of jacket.   *Embroidered sleeve of jacket.*

1. Fuse leaves to the jacket with iron-on adhesive, following manufacturer's instructions. Fuse three to the lower right sleeve, three to the top of the back and five to the front.

2. Outline stitch the leaves with two strands of brown floss.
3. Draw chalk lines from each leaf in a slightly curved pattern. Refer to the photos as guides.

The longest embroidered leaf lines are 11", except where leaves fall the full length of the sleeve. Since the design is meant to look like falling leaves, the lines don't have to be exact.

4. Embroider a running stitch from each leaf along the chalk line with two strands of floss.
5. Sew six bugle beads to the center line of each leaf.

Sewing the Front Trim

1. Press under ½" along both front edges.
2. Press under ½" along all four sides of the long plaid strips. Press strips in half.
3. Pin strips to the inside front edges, extending ¼" beyond the jacket edges.
4. Topstitch in place.
5. Separate the zipper. Pin it to the inside of the front trim with ⅛" of zipper visible beyond the teeth.
6. Topstitch the zipper in place.

The contrasting color of the zipper will add extra detail to the jacket.

Sewing the Side Seams

1. Fold your jacket right sides together along the underarm seam line. At the halfway point on the seam, measure 1" and mark.
2. From this point, draw a line gradually becoming ½" at either end of the seam.
3. Pin along this line and try the jacket on before continuing.

> If the jacket is too loose, add another ¼" to your measurement and redraw the line. If the jacket is too tight, reduce the line by ¼".

4. Sew seams. Finish seams. Press.

5. Press the hem under ½" along the jacket bottom.

6. Apply fusible web tape to the hem. Hem the jacket bottom with two rows of topstitching. Press.

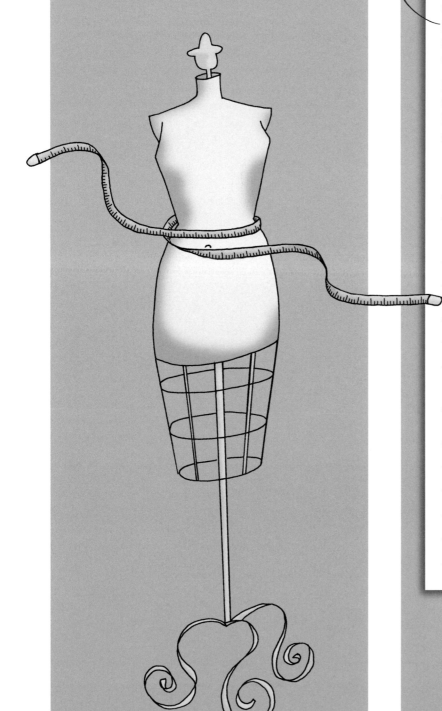

ACCENT, ALTER AND ACCESSORIZE!

Chanel is the term used to describe the box-shaped, hip-length, collarless jacket style that Coco Chanel made popular after adapting it from the cardigan sweater around 1930. Chanel-style jackets are often made of nubby fabrics and typically feature contrasting trim and patch pockets. This style is a good choice for slim and average size figures; it can also be flattering for women with long waists and small chests.

If you happen to wear jackets all the time and are looking for something different, try a pattern that includes at least one neutral color that you can wear with existing solid pieces.

— Diana

Accent

- Machine embroider an allover leaf design on the jacket with colored threads.

- Bead the neckband and lower jacket hem.

- Topstitch with contrasting thread.

Alter

- Change colors: Try using chocolate brown and gold.

- Shorten the jacket and sleeves, and add curved seaming for petites.

- Add shoulder pads for narrow shoulders.

Accessorize!

- Brown turtleneck

- Jeans

- Chocolate loafers

- Woof scarf

- Gloves

SNOWFLAKE SURPRISE!

If you live where the snow can begin in October and last until May, you want to stay warm while enjoying the charm of a wintery landscape. Cozy soft blue fleece paired with white boa trim and beads reflect the breathtaking beauty of the sparkling snow against the icy blue sky. To top it off, appliqué fleece snowflakes glitter with a simple but eye-catching bead design.

MATERIALS:

* 1 white sweatshirt
* 1⅓ yd. blue fleece
* 2 yd. white boa
* 1 package white E beads
* 1 package blue E beads
* 3 dozen 6mm crystal bicone faceted beads
* 3 large snaps
* Matching thread
* Sewing notions listed in Chapter One

PATTERNS:

Finished Length: 46"

Snowflake and Lower Front Curve Guide pieces from the Pattern Sheet "Snowflake Surprise!" is #13 on the Pattern Sheet

86

white Sweatshirt

cut along center line front

cut along ⌐ line

5"

cut off cuffs

cut off band ⤒

Snowflake Surprise
Long coat
Body Type: Tall Pear
White Sweatshirt: M
Appliqué
Beaded

CUTTING PLAN:

❋ Cut one 27" x 50" lower coat piece from fleece

❋ Cut three 3" x 58" front trim pieces from fleece

❋ Cut two 8" x 11" cuff pieces from fleece

❋ Cut one 6½" x 48" scarf piece from fleece

❋ Cut one 6" x 9" back tab piece from fleece

❋ Cut three white snowflakes from the bottom piece cut from the sweatshirt

❋ Cut two blue snowflakes from fleece

Reviewing Chapter One before you begin will be very helpful. Sew ½" seams with pieces right sides together unless otherwise indicated.

Cutting the Sweatshirt

1. Refer to the Inspiration Board for a cutting diagram for the sweatshirt. Cut off the band and cuffs.

2. Cut your sweatshirt open along the underarm seams.

3. Measure 5" down from the underarm seams. Cut the sweatshirt off along this line.

Back of the jacket.

Cutting the Lower Coat

1. Lay the lower coat fleece piece flat, wrong-side up. Place Lower Front Curve Guide along either end of the lower coat piece, matching the pattern piece ends to the edges of the fleece.

2. Draw and cut along this line to create a lower front curve on both ends.

3. Stay stitch along all four sides of the fleece.

Sewing the Curved Seams

1. Lay the coat completely flat, wrong side facing up. Place the Curve C guide along the back sleeve stitch line and draw a line along the curve. Repeat for the opposite side of the back.

2. Right sides together, fold along these lines and pin.

3. Measure and mark ½" in from this line at the seam line, narrowing to even with the seam line at the upper end.

4. Sew along this line. Repeat for the opposite side. Press.

5. Topstitch with contrasting or matching thread.

6. Fold the upper coat right sides together along the underarm seam line.

7. Sew seams. Finish and press.

Sewing the Coat Together

1. Run two lines of gathering stitches along the top edge of the lower coat.

2. Measure the lower coat piece to the upper coat piece edge. Pull the gathers evenly to fit the lower edge to the upper edge.

3. Push the gathers slightly so the gathers begin 3" in from the edges of the front piece.

4. Pin right sides together. Sew seam. Finish and press.

Adding Front Trim

1. Measure carefully from the neck ribbing to the lower edge of the coat, staying even with the upper side seam while going around the curve. Cut two pieces of binding plus 2" from this measurement.

2. Measure between these two points across the bottom edge and add 1". Cut a third piece of binding to this measurement.

3. Sew the pieces together end to end, with the shorter piece in the center.

Draw the curve for the front edge of the coat.

When sewing with fleece, use a ballpoint needle that will go between the fibers and prevent the fleece from being pushed into the needle plate. For a heavier topstitch effect, use two spools of thread through the needle as one.

4. Fold in half, wrong sides together. Press.

5. Begin pinning the binding to the coat at the neck edge ribbing right sides, with ½" extending beyond the ribbing.

6. Sew seam. Finish and press.

Sewing the Scarf

1. Cut a 3" fringe at both ends of the scarf.

2. Center the scarf with the center back of the neck.

3. Pin right sides together along the top of the ribbing, extending across the trim at the front.

4. Sew in place. Finish and press in half.

5. Pin the remaining edge of the scarf to the bindings on the inside edge of the neck.

6. Topstitch in place, leaving the rest of the scarf falling folded to front.

Sewing the Cuffs

1. Fold the cuff pieces in half, right sides together.

2. Sew along three sides, leaving a 2" opening on the long side to turn.

3. Try the coat on to determine sleeve length.

4. Slide the cuffs on the sleeve ends to check placement.

5. Remove the coat.

6. Pin the cuffs in place, matching the seams. Hand or machine stitch in place.

Adding Back Tab

1. Fold the back band piece in half, right sides together.

2. Sew seam, leaving a 2" opening.

3. Clip corners. Turn right sides out and press.

4. Topstitch all four sides.

5. Center the back tab in the back between the upper and lower coat pieces.

6. Pull in an extra 2" between the band ends. Pin.

7. Try the coat on to check how the back falls. Adjust fullness between the band ends by adding to or reducing the 2".

8. Sew the ends of the band in place.

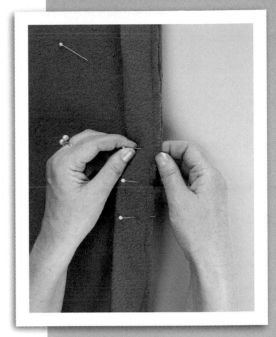

Step 5

Don't stretch the fleece when you are sewing around the front curve. If it is distorted at all when you finish, press thoroughly with steam and it should stay flat.

Snowflake Appliqué

1. Pin three white snowflakes to the lower coat front, approximately 2" apart.
2. Topstitch in place by hand or machine.
3. Pin the blue snowflake to the upper front of the coat and to the center back of the neck.
4. Topstitch in place.

Beading the Coat

1. Sew a white E bead in the center of each white snowflake and in the center of the blue snowflake at the back of the neck.

Step 2

2. Sew beads to the blue snowflake with a small running stitch, adding a bead with each stitch. Repeat for all four lines on the snowflake.

Step 3

3. Sew five beads in a snowflake pattern to the opposite ends of the back tab.

Step 4

4. Sew 8 to 12 groups of five beads in a snowflake pattern randomly to the scarf.

5. Sew white and blue E beads randomly to the scarf, around the snowflakes on the coat, and along the cuffs.

Adding Boa Trim

1. Measure around the neck edge and add 2". Cut.
2. Measure around the cuff and add 1". Cut two pieces.
3. Turn ends under 1" for the neck trim.
4. Turn ends under ½" for the cuff trim pieces.
5. Sew the boa trim by hand along the seam lines of the neck and cuffs.

ACCENT, ALTER AND ACCESSORIZE!

Accent

- Bead the coat with more E beads.
- Embroider a white snowflake design all over the lower coat.

Alter

- Change colors: Try red and white for the holidays.
- Shorten or lengthen for height. The coat can be shortened to the hip line.
- For a fuller bust, lengthen the top of the coat and use a darker color on top.
- Add pockets to the front.
- Replace the boa with white fur trim.

Accessorize!

- Cashmere sweater
- Navy wool pants
- Black boots
- White fur mittens

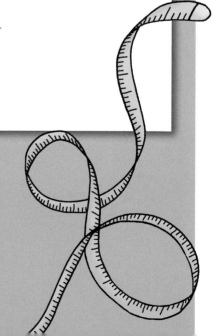

A LITTLE PINK

October is a month we celebrate with love by honoring and supporting breast cancer survivors and remembering those who are gone. Pink ribbons wave in the wind as survivors, daughters, sons, husbands, friends and many more run for the cure. Make this very warm and very pink jacket for someone special to snuggle up in after the run or while cheering from the side. This is truly a design from my heart to yours.

MATERIALS:

* 1 pink sweatshirt
* 1 yd. pink fleece
* 1 yd. pink flannel
* ¼ yd. ½"-wide pink grosgrain ribbon
* Iron-on adhesive tape
* Matching thread
* Sewing notions listed in Chapter One

PATTERNS:
Collar and Side Gore pieces from the Pattern Sheet
"A Little Pink" is #14 on the Pattern Sheet

Finished Length: 24"

CUTTING PLAN:

- ❀ Cut two 6" x 12" cuff pieces from fleece
- ❀ Cut two collar pieces from fleece
- ❀ Cut four gore pieces from fleece
- ❀ Cut two 5" x 25" front strip pieces from flannel
- ❀ Cut back lining from flannel*

Use the sweatshirt as a pattern. Refer to Cutting the Jacket Lining. Lining is optional.

Back of the jacket.

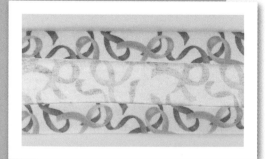

Steps 4 and 5

Reviewing Chapter One before you begin will be very helpful. Sew ½" seams with pieces right sides together unless otherwise indicated.

Cutting the Sweatshirt

1. Refer to the Inspiration Board for a cutting diagram for the sweatshirt. Remove the cuffs and band, leaving the stitching line attached. Set the band aside for ties.
2. Cut open along the underarm seam lines.
3. Lay the sweatshirt flat. Measure the center front line and cut.
4. Use the collar pattern piece as a guide to trim the neckline. Place the collar piece along the front of the sweatshirt, extending from the front edge to the shoulder seam and corresponding mark on the pattern piece. Draw a line along the inner collar edge between these points. Repeat for the opposite side.
5. Cut along this line. Repeat for the opposite side. The line will cut off some of the neckband, but leave the rest of the band because you will use it to finish the underside of the collar.

Cutting Jacket Lining

1. Lay the flannel right-side up. Lay the sweatshirt back flat, wrong-side up on the flannel. Draw lines on the flannel along the bottom, side seams to shoulder seams, adding ¼" extra at this line and at the neckline.
2. Cut along these lines.

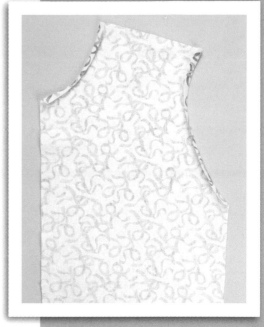

Steps 1 and 2

Sewing Jacket Lining

1. Finish the edges of the lining piece along the neck, shoulder seams and to the underarm seam line.
2. Pin lining along all edges, and sew along both side seams at ¼".
3. Topstitch across the shoulder seam.

> With flat lining, it is important to wash both fabrics to check for compatibility, as they will be treated as one.

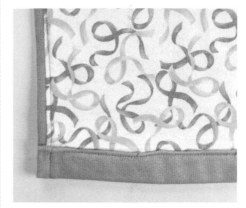

Finished inside edges of the lining.

4. Cut the band in half. Sew across one end of each piece. Turn the pieces wrong-side out to use as ties. Press. Topstitch open ends shut.
5. Pin this end of the tie along the front, just below the curve where the collar will begin.

Sewing Side Gores

1. Align the gore pieces right sides together with the bottom edge of the side seams, both front and back.
2. Pin in place.
3. Sew in place with ½" seam. Finish seam and press.

Finished gore insert seams.

Sewing the Jacket

1. Press ½" along both sleeve ends to the right side of the jacket.
2. Topstitch along the sleeve ends.
3. Fold the jacket right sides together, aligning underarms, shoulders and gore seams. Pin.
4. Sew underarm seams. Finish and press.

Sewing the Collar

1. Pin collar pieces right sides together. Sew seam all around, leaving an opening to turn.
2. Trim corners and seam. Turn collar and press.
3. Topstitch collar on three sides except for the lower edge.
4. Pin the right-side bottom edge of the collar to the wrong-side lower edge of the neckband.
5. Sew along the bottom edge, using the topstitch line as a guide. Press seam.
6. Flip the collar to the right side of your jacket. This technique will give the collar body.
7. Hand-stitch ribbing to the collar lining to give the underside of the collar a finished look.

Sewing the Cuffs

1. Fold 1" under along both sides of the cuff pieces. Press.
2. Topstitch ½" along both sides of the cuff pieces.
3. Fold the cuffs in half, wrong sides together. Sew seam. Finish seam and press.
4. Try jacket on to determine sleeve length.
5. Slide the cuffs on the sleeve ends to check placement.
6. Remove the jacket.
7. Pin cuffs in place, matching seams. Hand or machine stitch in place.

Finishing the Jacket

1. Press hem under ¼". Press under 1" again.
2. Apply fusible web to the hem.
3. Topstitch along the hemline. Press.
4. Loop a pink ribbon and sew to collar.

ACCENT, ALTER AND ACCESSORIZE!

If you happen to wear jackets all the time and are looking for something different, try a pattern that includes at least one neutral color that you can wear with existing solid pieces.

— Diana

Accent

- Machine embroider a ribbon design all over the jacket, using the flannel lining as a pattern.
- Quilt the collar and cuffs along the ribbon pattern lines.

Alter

- Add a band of fleece along the bottom to increase length.
- Remove the arms to make a cozy vest.
- Create the jacket in a sweatshirt sized for larger body types.
- Cut a strip of fleece and make a simple but warm headband.

Accessorize!

- Cream turtleneck
- Jeans
- Ballet flats
- Cream gloves

HOLIDAY CHEER

This rich, burgundy bolero-style jacket can be dressed up or down. It is equally stunning with a long velvet skirt or wool pants and scarf. Wear it to an office party or holiday gathering, and show off your quilting and embellishing skills with this gorgeous, one-of-a-kind jacket.

MATERIALS:

- ❈ 1 burgundy sweatshirt
- ❈ ⅔ yd. paisley fabric A
- ❈ ⅔ yd. tree fabric B
- ❈ 1 fat quarter holiday print fabric C
- ❈ 1 fat quarter red plaid fabric D
- ❈ ½ skein red/green fashion yarn
- ❈ ¼ skein gold/brown fashion yarn*
- ❈ Iron-on gold #16 braid
- ❈ 1 yd. ⅜" gold/black trim
- ❈ 1 yd. ⅜" green trim
- ❈ 1 antique gold closure
- ❈ 2 pkg. iron-on adhesive
- ❈ Matching thread
- ❈ Sewing notions listed in Chapter One

*_Same yarn used in "For the Animal in You," pg. 73._

Finished Length: 23"

PATTERNS:
Curve C Guide and Sleeve Flounce pieces from the Pattern Sheet
"Holiday Cheer" is #15 on the Pattern Sheet

CUTTING PLAN:

❋ Cut three 3" x 44" ruffle pieces from fabric A

❋ Cut one 3" x 44" collar piece from fabric A

❋ Cut two sleeve flounce pieces from fabric A

❋ Cut two sleeve flounce lining pieces from fabric B

❋ Cut crazy quilt pieces from ABCD, according to the instructions

Reviewing Chapter One before you begin will be very helpful. Sew ½" seams with pieces right sides together unless otherwise indicated.

Back of the jacket.

Step 6

Cutting the Sweatshirt

1. Refer to the Inspiration Board for a cutting diagram for the sweatshirt. Begin by removing the bottom band and cuffs.

2. Cut open along the underarm seam lines.

3. Lay sweatshirt flat, wrong-side up. Measure 3" from the sleeve seam line. Cut this portion off.

4. Measure and cut 3" off the bottom of the sweatshirt.

5. Measure and draw the center line. Cut along this line.

6. Line up the bolero front curve guide (edge of flounce) along the front edge of the sweatshirt. Draw a line, and cut along this line for the front curve. Repeat for the other front edge of the sweatshirt.

7. Stay stitch around all raw edges.

Sewing the Curve C Seams

1. Lay the jacket completely flat, wrong-side up. Place Curve C guide along the back sleeve stitch line, and draw a line along the curve to the bottom edge. Repeat for the opposite side of the back.

2. Right sides together, fold along these lines.

3. Measure and mark ¼" in from this line at the lower edge. Pin at this point, narrowing to even with the seam line.

4. Sew along this line. Repeat for the opposite side. Press.

5. Topstitch.

Crazy Quilting the Jacket

1. Begin by fusing 8" squares of fabrics ABCD to the adhesive.

Step 2

2. Cut rounded rectangular shapes and triangles approximately 4" x 5" from each of the four fabrics ABCD.

Steps 3 and 4

3. Arrange these pieces, alternating fabrics and shapes, and overlapping ⅛" on one shoulder. Align fabric along the ribbed neck edge.

4. Trim curves along neck.

5. Following manufacturer's instructions, iron the pieces in place.

6. Continue cutting and arranging pieces of fabric until the design is complete from shoulder to shoulder.

Crazy quilting is a good way to use up scraps of fabrics and trims, or fat quarters of specialty fabrics. It involves cutting pieces in random shapes, fusing them in place, and adding stitching and trims to embellish the pattern. In this jacket, machine stitching was used over yarn for an interesting effect, but hand-embroidered stitches would also be lovely. Choose which method you prefer, and have fun with the design using these instructions as a guideline. The crazy quilt design is asymmetrical over the shoulders, measuring 10½" down one shoulder and 5½" over the other. The design is 4" to 4½" wide at the center back.

7. Cut 18" pieces of yarn, and place at the end of the overlapping fabrics next to the collar. Stitch the yarn in place with a small zigzag or embroidery stitch, continuing along another fabric section. Keep the ribbed collar out of the way while stitching down yarn. Folding the ribbed neck down later results in a better finish.

8. Cut more yarn, overlapping one piece ¼" to the next piece. Continue until all of the overlapped sections are covered.

9. Measure the length across the alternating sections of fabric, and cut pieces of trim these lengths.

10. Stitch trim pieces across the center of the alternating fabric sections.

Steps 11, 12

11. Begin on the left side of the jacket 2" from the lower edge, unwinding braid from the

spool. It will tend to fall in loops on the jacket. Arrange in a random pattern up the front of the jacket.

12. Pin and iron in place, following manufacturer's instructions.

13. Continue around the neck of the jacket, looping on fabric sections without trim. Finish at the end of the last fabric section on the opposite shoulder.

Crazy Quilting the Sleeve Flounce

1. Fuse 6"-square pieces of fabrics to BCD. Cut three approximately 5" by 3" pieces from each fabric and one extra from C, making a combination of uneven triangles and narrow rectangles.

2. Arrange fabric pieces on the right sides of the flounce, overlapping ⅛" and leaving some sections open so the flounce fabric A is visible. Repeat for the second flounce. Trim pieces extending over the flounce edge.

Step 2

3. Following manufacturer's instructions, iron the pieces in place.

4. Cut 18" pieces of yarn, and place them at the end of the overlapping fabrics next to the flounce edge. Select a small zigzag or embroidery stitch, and stitch yarn in place, continuing along another fabric section.

5. Cut more yarn, overlapping one piece ¼" to the next piece. Continue until all overlapped sections are covered.

6. Measure across sections of fabric approximately 6" and cut three pieces each of both trims.

Step 7

7. Stitch trims every third section across the center of the fabric sections.

8. Align the flounce lining and flounce fronts right sides together. Sew a ¼" seam on three sides, leaving the top open. Clip corners. Turn and press carefully.

9. Pin the flounce right sides together to the end of the sleeves. Repeat for the second flounce.

10. Sew seam.

11. Begin from the lower edge of the right flounce, unwinding the braid from the spool. It will tend to fall in loops on the flounce. Arrange in a random looped pattern up the center of the sleeve to the front of the shoulder with a narrow quilted pattern.

12. Pin and iron in place, following manufacturer's instructions.

13. Apply loops of braid to the opposite flounce.

Sewing the Side Seams

1. Fold the jacket right sides together along the underarm seam line. At the halfway point on the seam, measure 1" and mark.

2. From this point, draw a line gradually becoming even with the opposite ends of the seam.

3. Pin along this line and try your jacket on before continuing.

> If the jacket is too loose, add another ¼" to your measurement and redraw the line. If the jacket is too tight, reduce the line by ¼". This seaming will give the jacket a flattering hourglass shape.

4. Sew seams. Finish and press.

Sewing the Ruffle

1. Sew three ruffle pieces together, end to end.

2. Fold in half right sides together, and sew across the opposite ends. Trim and press.

3. Fold the entire piece in half, wrong sides together, and run two lines of gathering stitches ⅛" and ¼" in from the raw edge.

> Break up the gathering stitches at each section to make pulling gathers easier.

4. Pull gathers to fit from one end of the neck ribbing of the jacket to the opposite side. Pin.

5. Sew. Finish seam and press.

6. Topstitch.

Sewing the Collar Ruffle

1. Align and sew the remaining ruffle pieces together along both long sides.

2. Turn and press with red tree print extending ½" beyond the paisley print.

3. Fold ends in ½", press and topstitch.

Step 4

4. Sew two lines of gathering stitches ⅛" and ¼" in from edge.

5. Pull gathers to fit the neck edge.

6. Pin the collar ruffle edge to the right side of the neck ribbing seam line. Sew. Press.

7. Fold the neck ribbing over to the inside.

8. Topstitch the collar ruffle along the neck edge.

9. Hand-sew the lower edge of the ribbing in place along the neck.

Adding the Yarn Braid

1. Cut six pieces of 60" yarn, three of red and three of gold.
2. Knot and pin yarn ends together to something stable, like a chair.
3. Twist together tightly, and let the yarn twist back on itself.

Step 4

4. Pin along the collar edge, and sew in place by hand. As you sew, use red thread looping over and under the braid for an extra accent.
5. Cut three 60" yarn pieces of each color again, and twist together several inches at a time.
6. Pin at the neck edge and continue to twist along the ruffle front edge. Hand-sew in place.
7. Repeat the last two steps for the opposite front side of the jacket. Join the ends together neatly, and sew.
8. Tuck the ends of the braid at the neck edge under the trim. Sew the closure at either side of the ruffled collar where the trims join.
9. Cut three 30" strands of each red and gold.
10. Twist together, forming a braid.
11. Measure down 4" on the right front side next to the ruffle. Pin.

Step 12

12. Shape both ends into a swirl design. Pin and stitch in place.
13. Cut three 30" pieces, two red and one gold.
14. Twist together, pin and sew to the flounce edge. Trim ends.

ACCENT, ALTER AND ACCESSORIZE!

Wearing all one color from head to toe draws the eye up and down and makes you look tall and thin. You can match the same color from head to toe, or opt for slight variations of the same color family. Light and bright colors will make you look bigger; dark and muted colors will make you look smaller.

— Diana

Accent

- Crazy quilt the entire jacket.
- Machine embroider with gold thread.
- Add bead accents to the quilted sections.

Alter

- Lengthen your jacket without cutting an extra piece off of the bottom.
- Omit the ruffle and add a flat band of fabric trim.
- For a fuller bust, add extra closures.
- For a leaner look, keep the bottom band of fabric very close to the main jacket color.

Accessorize!

- Green velour sweater
- Black wool pants
- Leather boots
- Velvet purse

CHAPTER FIVE

A special occasion, whether it is a party, an anniversary or a dinner out, calls for a dressy outfit. The jackets in this chapter sparkle, shimmer and shine, and make you feel and look sensational. When a party invitation comes, you know that you will have something wonderful to wear!

ELEGANT SPLENDOR

SILVER SHIMMER

I was browsing through the fabric aisles, and this absolutely stunning sheer fabric with flocked and silver roses caught my eye. Elegant jackets need elegant fabrics, so I bought it not quite knowing how it would work out. With the sweatshirt cut into angles, it transformed into an easy-to-make shimmering evening coat! Throw this on with a satin cami and black evening pants, and you are gorgeous and ready to go! Now where is that carriage?

MATERIALS:

* 1 black sweatshirt
* 2⅓ yd. 60"-wide black sheer fabric with allover pattern
* ⅔ yd. 1½"-wide black satin ribbon
* 2⅓ yd. 1"-wide black grosgrain ribbon
* 3 yd. ¼"-wide black and silver beaded trim
* 1 package ¼" double-fold bias tape
* 3" black ¼"-wide cord
* 1 silver ½" button
* Matching thread
* Sewing notions listed in Chapter One

Finished Length: 36"

102

Black Sweatshirt

cut off neck

cut along center front line

cut along dotted lines

cut off cuffs

cut off band

Silver Shimmer
3/4 coat
Body Type: Apple
Black Sweatshirt: L
Layered Design
Silver Trim

CUTTING PLAN:

❁ Cut black grosgrain ribbon in half

❁ Cut two 14" pieces from silver beaded trim

❁ Cut two 20" pieces from silver beaded trim

Reviewing Chapter One before you begin will be very helpful. Sew ½" seams with pieces right sides together unless otherwise indicated.

Cutting the Sweatshirt

1. Refer to the Inspiration Board for the basic cutting diagram for the sweatshirt. Begin by removing the bottom band, cuffs and neckband.

2. Cut open along the underarm seam lines. Do not cut the center front open yet.

3. With ruler and rotary cutter, straighten all ends.

4. Lay the sweatshirt flat, wrong-side up. Mark the center points on the bottom edges of the front, back and both sleeves with chalk.

5. Beginning with the front center point, line up the ruler at the center point, angling it to the underarm seam point. Draw a line. Repeat for the opposite front side, both sleeves and back (the lines will resemble a star).

6. Draw a center front line, and at the back bottom center point, draw a line 11" up the center back. Cut along all the lines except for the center front line, which will be cut later.

Back of the coat.

Steps 4, 5 and 6

103

Step 7

7. Measure 14" up from the center bottom point along the lower-back angle. Begin sewing bias tape at this point down to the end point, up to the center point, down, and then up the opposite back angle to the 14" mark. This gives the inside lower slit a nice, finished look.

Steps 3 and 4

Cutting the Fabric

1. Lay the sheer fabric flat, wrong-side up. Use the cut sweatshirt as a pattern and lay it over the top of the fabric, wrong-side up and centered on all sides.
2. Pin the sheer fabric to the sweatshirt at the neck, along both sides of the center front line, sleeve ends and center back.
3. Measure 6" on either side of the center sleeve point for sleeve width of 12". Draw a straight line from the 6" measurement to the underarm seam. Repeat for both sleeves.
4. Draw a line from the underarm seam straight down to the end of the fabric at the front and back for side seams.
5. Cut along the sleeve and side lines.
6. Cut up the center front line through both the sheer and the sweatshirt.
7. Cut around the collar through both the sheer and the sweatshirt.
8. At the center back line, cut only 5" for a slit through the sheer.

Assembling the Coat Body

1. Make sure the sheer fabric is completely smooth and unwrinkled under the sweatshirt.
2. Pin or baste along the diagonal lines of the sleeves, front and back.
3. Stitch close to the edge around the collar opening and down the center fronts.

4. Stitch close to the edge along all sleeve diagonal lines from the center point to the underarm seam line.
5. Stitch along both front diagonal lines from the center point to the underarm.
6. Stitch along both back diagonal lines from the underarm to where the bias tape begins.
7. Clip all threads. Press (place the sweatshirt side under the iron).

Step 4

When sewing along the diagonal lines, keep re-checking the coat to make sure that both layers stay smooth.

Finishing the Front and Collar

1. Press under ½" along both sides of the front.
2. Pin 1"-wide ribbon to the inside along both edges, extending ½" beyond the edge. Topstitch in place.
3. Press the neck edge over ¼" to the right side.
4. Measure the neck edge, adding 2½". Cut the 1½"- wide satin ribbon to this measurement.
5. Press the ends of the ribbon under ¼" and then 1" again.
6. Pin the ribbon to the neck, beginning at the front edge.
7. Topstitch close to ribbon edge around neck.
8. Clip all threads.
9. Sew a button to the end of the ribbon collar.
10. Make a loop with the cord. Check to see that it fits over the button.
11. Hand-stitch loop ends to the inside of the opposite side of the collar.

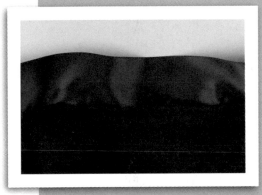

Step 7

Applying the Trim

1. Lay the coat out flat, right-side up.
2. Draw a straight line from the shoulder seam to the underarm seam. Repeat for the other front side.
3. Pin a 14" piece of beaded trim along this line from the ribbon collar line to ½" short of the underarm seam. Trim off any excess.
4. Hand-stitch these two pieces in place with matching thread.
5. Pin the two 20" pieces from ½" beyond the underarm seam, along the sewn front diagonal lines, and to the front edge.
6. Hand-stitch in place.
7. Pin the remaining piece of beaded trim to the collar edge.
8. Hand-stitch in place.

Sewing the Seams and Hems

1. Fold the coat right sides together and place a few pins in the underarm seams.
2. Try the coat on to determine sleeve and hem length. The sleeves will need a 1" hem and bottom hem will need 1½". Trim off any excess, if needed.
3. Press under ½", then ½" again on the ends of the sleeves.
4. Topstitch the sleeve hems.
5. With right sides together, line up the sleeve and underarm side seams. Pin.
6. Sew seams. Finish seams and press.

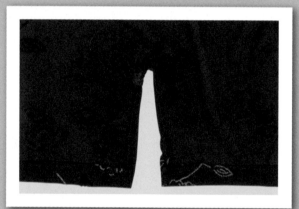

Back slit and hem.

7. Press hem under ¼", including the back slit. Press under 1", excluding the slit.
8. Topstitch the hem, including the slit.

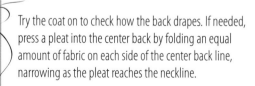

Try the coat on to check how the back drapes. If needed, press a pleat into the center back by folding an equal amount of fabric on each side of the center back line, narrowing as the pleat reaches the neckline.

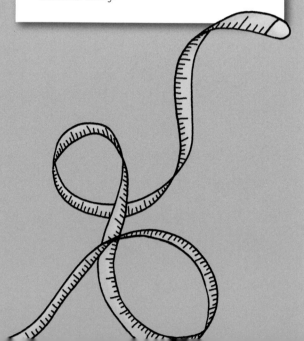

ACCENT, ALTER AND ACCESSORIZE!

Wearing all one color from head to toe draws the eye up and down and makes you look tall and thin. You can match the same color from head to toe, or opt for slight variations of the same color family. Light and bright colors will make you look bigger; dark and muted colors will make you look smaller.

— Diana

Accent

- Use plain, sheer fabric and machine embroider your own design.
- Add rhinestones to the collar.
- Add matching rhinestone buttons.

Alter

- Change colors: Try using a pastel sweatshirt and matching sheer for spring.
- To create a jacket, shorten and cut 2" beyond the diagonal points.
- If the coat is too wide under the underarm, sew this seam narrower and trim off excess.

Accessorize!

- Silver cami
- Black flare pants
- Silver slingbacks
- Chandelier earrings

VAVOOM!

Vavoom is right in this arresting blazer with shawl collar. Quilted, specialty braid and rhinestone accents plus vibrant batik butterfly fabric in reverse appliqué combine with dynamite flair. This beautiful jacket is just waiting for that very special occasion!

MATERIALS:

* 1 green sweatshirt
* ¾ yd. batik fabric
* ⅓ yd. striped fabric
* 3 yd. orange bead trim
* 8" x 45" quilt batting
* 1 package each 3mm fuchsia, purple, turquoise and lime green hot-fix rhinestones
* 1 spool each fine copper and medium metallic blue iron-on braid
* 6 yd. variegated fiber trim
* 1 skein green embroidery floss
* Matching thread
* Hot-fix crystal applicator
* Mini iron
* Basting glue stick
* Sewing notions listed in Chapter One

Finished Length: 25"

PATTERNS:
Collar, Curve C Guide and Lower Curve Guide pieces from the Pattern Sheet
"Vavoom!" is #17 on the Pattern Sheet

CUTTING PLAN:

* Cut two 4" x 12½" cuff pieces from batik fabric

* Cut two 4" x 12½" cuff pieces from striped fabric

* Cut twelve butterflies from batik fabric*

* Cut two collar pieces from batik fabric

* Cut one collar piece from quilt batting

* Cut twelve 12" pieces of blue iron-on braid

* Cut eight 24" pieces of copper iron-on braid

* Cut two 13" cuff pieces from beaded trim

Leave ½" border around the butterflies.

Back of the coat.

Reviewing Chapter One before you begin will be very helpful. Sew ½" seams with pieces right sides together unless otherwise indicated.

Cutting the Sweatshirt

1. Refer to the Inspiration Board for a cutting diagram for the sweatshirt. Remove the bottom band, cuffs and neckband.
2. Cut open along the underarm seam lines.
3. Lay the sweatshirt flat. Measure the center front line and cut.

4. Use the collar pattern piece as a guide to trim the neckline. Place the collar piece along the front of the sweatshirt, extending from the front edge to the shoulder seam and corresponding mark on the pattern piece. Draw a line along the inner collar edge between these points. Repeat for the opposite side.
5. Cut along this line. Repeat for the opposite side.
6. Place the curve guide along the lower edge. Draw line and cut. Repeat for the opposite side.

Steps 4 and 5

Sewing the Curved Seams

1. Lay the jacket completely flat, wrong-side up. Place the Curve C guide along the back sleeve stitch line, and draw a line along the curve to the bottom edge. Repeat for the opposite side of the back.
2. Right sides together, fold along these lines.
3. Measure and mark ¼" from the fold, beginning at the lower edge of the jacket. Pin at this point, narrowing to even with the sleeve stitch line.
4. Sew along this line. Repeat for the opposite side. Press.

Making the Reverse Appliqué

Choose a shape that is easy to sew around and fabric with a design that you can see on the wrong side.

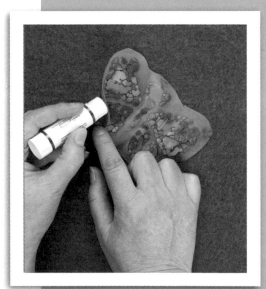

Step 1

1. With a basting stick, apply appliqué wrong-side up to the wrong side of the jacket. Apply the stick just around the outside edge.
2. Apply two butterflies to the fronts and sleeves. Apply four butterflies to the back.
3. From the wrong side, sew around the flowers, following the outline of the pattern. Repeat for all the butterflies.
4. From the right side, carefully cut the sweatshirt away from the butterflies. Begin by making a small slit in the center.
5. Cut close to the stitching on all the butterflies. Press.

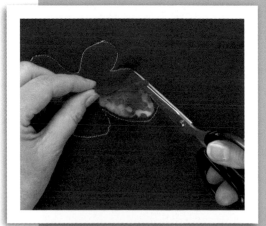

Steps 4 and 5

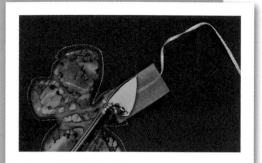

Steps 2 and 3

Steps 4 and 5

Applying Crystals and Iron-on Braid

1. Apply four of each crystal color to the butterflies according to manufacturer's instructions.
2. Place each blue iron-on braid piece from the stitched edge of the butterfly and swirl onto the jacket. The braid will swirl off the spool on its own. Work with one piece at a time.
3. Heat the mini iron. Use a pressing cloth, and begin ironing the thread in place. Repeat for all butterflies.
4. Swirl the copper pieces in a random pattern on the jacket. Iron each piece in place.

Sewing the Cuffs

1. Pin the cuff pieces right sides together, one batik and one striped.
2. Sew along both long sides.
3. Turn right-side out. Press with the stripe extending 1" beyond the batik.
4. Pin and sew the beaded trim to the cuffs on the reverse side of the striped end.
5. Topstitch the variegated trim along the lower edge of the cuffs.
6. Press the sleeve ends ½" to the right side.
7. Measure the cuffs along the sleeve ends. Sew the cuffs, extending ½" beyond the sleeve end. Trim the cuff or sleeve if uneven.
8. Pin cuffs in place.
9. Add trim along the upper edge and striped seam line of cuffs. Topstitch in place.

Sewing the Side Seams

1. Fold the jacket right sides together along the underarm seam line. Mark the halfway point at the side seam, measure 1" in and mark.
2. From the halfway point, draw a line narrowing gradually to ½" at either end of the seam.
3. Pin along this line and try the jacket on before continuing.
4. If the jacket is too loose, add another ¼" to your measurement and redraw the line. If the jacket is too tight, reduce the line by ¼".
5. Sew seams. Finish and press.
6. Press ½" under along the entire edge of the jacket.
7. Apply trim ⅛" in from the pressed edge, and topstitch in place around the entire jacket.

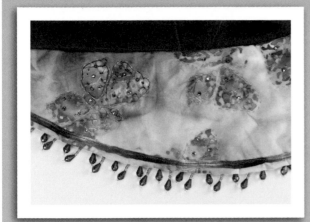

Finished collar.

Sewing the Collar

1. Pin the collar pieces right sides together, with the quilt batting piece on the wrong side. Sew seam all around, leaving a 2" opening to turn.
2. Trim corners and seam. Turn collar and press.
3. Sew beads to the underside of the collar along the outer edge.
4. Apply trim to the collar, and topstitch in place on the outside edge of the collar.
5. Quilt around all butterflies on the collar front with two strands of green floss.
6. Heat hot-fix applicator and apply rhinestones to the butterflies on the collar.
7. Match centers and pin the right-side bottom edge of the collar to the wrong side of the neck.
8. Sew in place along the bottom edge, using the topstitch line as a guide. Press seam.
9. Flip the collar to the right side of your jacket. This technique will give the collar body.
10. Stitch in the ditch along collar.

Sewing the Ties

1. Fold ties in half, right sides together.
2. Sew along two sides, leaving one end open. Clip corners. Turn.
3. Fold open end in ½" and press.
4. Apply trim and topstitch along both edges of each tie.
5. Try the jacket on and mark where ties are to be placed in the center of the jacket.

6. Pin ties ½" to the inside fronts of the jacket. Sew in place at the topstitch line.

ACCENT, ALTER AND ACCESSORIZE!

A blazer is a lightweight, loose-fitting, tailored jacket, typically with a shawl collar and notched lapel. Classic versions hit anywhere from mid-hip to the bottom of the buttocks, and because of its simple line, it can be worn easily by most figure types. If you're petite or plus size, opt for a color that allows you to wear the blazer as part of a monochromatic ensemble to make you look taller and slimmer.

— Diana

Accent

- Add beaded trim to the bottom of the jacket.
- Quilt and bead collar and cuffs more extensively.

Alter

- Change colors: Try using chocolate brown and ivory.
- Use snaps sewn along the neck edge to make the collar detachable.
- For a petite, make the blazer shorter.
- Add side and sleeve gore pattern pieces to create a fuller jacket.

Accessorize!

- Silk blouse
- Teal flare skirt
- Rust satin heels
- Drop earrings
- Evening bag

CELESTIAL CHARM

Be a shining star in this elegant, asymmetrical wrap jacket. The celestial fabric inspired the name and design. Tiny gold studs sparkle along the border and cuffs, and a rich satin ribbon belts the jacket with a classy final element. Beaded fringe completes this evening topper, perfect for any special occasion!

MATERIALS:

* 1 black sweatshirt
* ⅓ yd. orange celestial fabric A
* ½ yd. coordinating celestial fabric B
* 2 yd. 1"-wide gold satin ribbon
* 2 yd. 1"-wide rust satin ribbon
* 1 pkg. gold hot-fix rhinestuds
* 1 pkg. 1½"-wide orange beaded trim
* 1 yd. black embroidery floss
* 1 large black snap
* Hot-fix crystal applicator
* Matching thread
* Sewing notions listed in Chapter One

Finished Length: 26"

PATTERN:
Curve C Guide piece on the Pattern Sheet
"Celestial Charm" is #18 on the Pattern Sheet

112

Black Sweatshirt

cut off neck

cut along front line

2/3

cut off 4"

cut off cuffs

cut off band

celestial charm

3/4 Sleeve Wrap

Body Type: Petite

Black Sweatshirt: M

Asymmetrical cut

Embellished

Satin Belt

CUTTING PLAN:

❋ Cut two 2½" x 36" front trim strips from fabric A

❋ Cut two 2½" x 36" front trim strips from fabric B

❋ Cut two 4" x 13" cuff strips from fabric A

❋ Cut two 4" x 13" cuff strips from fabric B

❋ Cut one 5½" x 45" bottom border strip from fabric B

Reviewing Chapter One before you begin will be very helpful. Sew ½" seams with pieces right sides together unless otherwise indicated.

Cutting the Sweatshirt

1. Refer to the Inspiration Board for a cutting diagram for the sweatshirt. Begin by removing the band, cuffs and neckband.

2. Cut open along the side seam lines.

3. Measure ⅔ over on the front of the sweatshirt, and draw a straight line. Cut.

Back of the jacket.

Step 4

Step 6

4. Place the upper edge of the Curve C guide along the front at the ⅔ line. Draw a line and cut.

5. Measure and cut 4" off the ends of the sleeves.

Sewing the Border

1. Measure the lower edge of the jacket. Add ¾" to each front measurement and 1" to the back measurement.

2. Cut three lower pieces according to these measurements from a 5½" x 45" bottom strip.

3. Right sides together, fold the pieces in half lengthwise. Sew along both long sides and one end.

4. Clip corners. Turn right-side out.

5. Fold the opposite short sides in ½" and press all pieces thoroughly.

6. Right sides together, pin the border pieces to the bottom of the sweatshirt, leaving ¼" at the seam lines.

7. Sew in place. Press seams down.

8. Topstitch along all three bottom border pieces.

Sewing the Front Trim

1. Right sides together, sew the front strips together to make two long strips.

2. Right sides together, sew the front strips together on both long sides to create a tube.

3. Turn the tube right-side out. Press unevenly, with B print extending ½" beyond A to create a double border.

4. Measure the border along the front edge, centering the seam at the back of the neck.

5. Add ½" to either end, and cut off any excess.

6. Press ends in ½".

7. Pin the front border to the jacket front, right sides together.

8. Sew in place. Press thoroughly with the seam toward the trim.

9. Topstitch the front edge border.

Because sweatshirts are stretchy in nature, they may appear to be distorted and out of shape. A thorough press with steam will usually return the desired shape. Repeat if necessary. It is important to press thoroughly with every step.

Sewing the Cuffs

1. Right sides together, pin the cuff pieces AB, long sides together.

2. Sew along both long sides.

3. Turn right-side out. Press, with B extending ½" beyond A.

4. Measure the cuffs along the sleeve ends. Sew the cuffs to the sleeve ends, extending ½" beyond the sleeve end. Trim if needed.

5. Cut two pieces of beaded trim ½" shorter than the cuff.

6. Pin the beaded trim to the wrong-side bottom edge of the cuff, with the satin edge extending ¼" beyond the edge.

7. Pin cuffs to the right sides of the sleeve ends, extending ½" beyond the sleeve edge.

8. Topstitch in place along both edges.

9. Apply gold studs to the pattern elements along the sleeves and front border.

If the satin edge of the trim does not work with your jacket, sew it so the edge does not show beyond the cuff. In this jacket, the satin edge matched the satin belt perfectly.

Step 7

Sewing the Seams

1. Fold the jacket right sides together along the underarm seam line. At the halfway point on the seam, measure 1" and mark.

2. From this point, draw a line gradually becoming even with the end edges.

3. Pin along this line and try the jacket on before continuing.

4. Sew seams and trim. Finish seams and press.

If the jacket is too loose, add another ¼" to your measurement and redraw the line. If jacket is too tight, reduce the line by ¼".

Finishing the Jacket

1. Overlap the long edges of ribbon ¼" and topstitch.

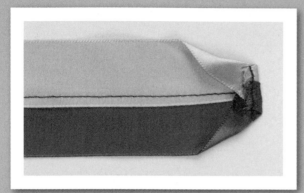

Steps 2 and 3

2. Press the lower ½" sides of the ribbon belt in to the center of the short ends of ribbon.

3. Press the short ends of the ribbon belt under ½". Topstitch across each end.

4. Try the jacket on to determine snap placement. Sew a snap in place on the front border.

5. Tie the ribbon belt around your jacket, just under the bust, to determine belt loop placement (approximately 3" below the underarm).

6. Use six strands of floss and knot. Secure the knot to the inside seam.

7. Take a needle through to the right side of the seam.

8. Measure down 2" and take the needle back through the seam to the inside. Secure the floss and trim excess floss. Repeat for the opposite seam.

9. Place the ribbon belt through loops.

ACCENT, ALTER AND ACCESSORIZE!

Opt for a monochromatic look (all one color) to appear slimmer and taller.

— Diana

Accent

- With gold thread, machine embroider an allover celestial design on the black jacket.

- Bead the front band with seed and bugle beads.

- Add a beaded fringe to the bottom of the jacket for extra sparkle.

Alter

- Change colors: Try using white and gold.

- This jacket can work for all body types.

- Create the jacket in a right-sized sweatshirt for larger body types.

- V-neck and three-quarter length sleeves visually elongate all body types.

- For a fuller bust, add more snaps.

- For fuller hips, make sure the bottom band does not hit the widest part of the hips — shorten or lengthen the jacket slightly.

- For a leaner look, keep the bottom band of fabric very close to the main jacket color.

Accessorize!

- Gold cami

- Black evening skirt

- Gold sandals

- Velvet clutch

CRYSTAL CHANDELIER

The wand has waved, the end of the fairy tale has come, and Cinderella is off to the ball in this dazzling coat. Silver and white ruffles highlight an asymmetrical hem and three-quarter length sleeves. Ribbon embroidery details the exquisite neckline of this dazzling garment, fit for every princess. Grab those glass slippers and ride off to the ball — the Prince is waiting!

MATERIALS:

- 1 white sweatshirt
- 3¾ yd. white and silver fabric
- 4 yd. ¼-wide silver trim
- 4 yd. ¼"-wide white satin ribbon
- 1½" rhinestone button
- 2 snaps
- White embroidery floss
- Matching thread
- Crewel needle
- Sewing notions listed in Chapter One

Finished Length: 40"

PATTERNS:

Curved C Guide and Lower Front Curve Guide pieces from the Pattern Sheet
"Crystal Chandelier" is #19 on the Pattern Sheet

CUTTING PLAN:

- ✱ Cut two 30" x 44" lower pieces from fabric
- ✱ Cut six 6" x 44" ruffle pieces from fabric
- ✱ Cut two 6" x 44" sleeve pieces from fabric
- ✱ Cut four 6" x 20" belt pieces lengthwise from fabric

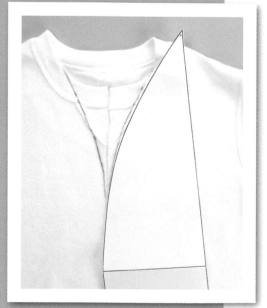

Back of the coat.

Step 6

Reviewing Chapter One before you begin will be very helpful. Sew ½" seams with pieces right sides together unless otherwise indicated.

Cutting the Sweatshirt

1. Refer to the Inspiration Board for a cutting diagram for the sweatshirt. Cut off the band and cuffs.
2. Cut the sweatshirt open along the underarm seams.
3. Measure and cut 6" off sleeves.
4. Measure 5" down from the underarm seams. Cut the sweatshirt off along this line.
5. Cut off the neckband ½" above the stitch line.
6. Measure ⅔ over on the front of the jacket. Place the upper edge of the Curve C guide along the front at the ⅔ mark. Draw a line.
7. Cut along this curved line.

Cutting the Lower Coat

1. Align both lower pieces together. One will be the lining.
2. Fold the pieces in half together. Pin along the edges to hold together.
3. Pin the Lower Front Curve Guide along the bottom outside edges of the fabric, matching x's on the Guide to outside edges of the fabric.
4. Cut through all four layers along this curved edge.

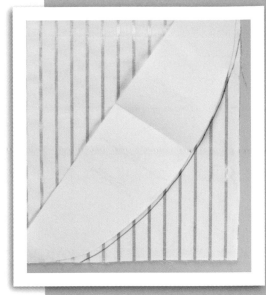

Step 3

Sewing the Lower Coat

1. Sew four ruffle pieces together end to end.
2. Fold in half, right sides together, and sew across the opposite ends. Trim and press.
3. Fold the entire piece in half, wrong sides together, and run two lines of gathering stitches ⅛" and ¼" in from the raw edge.
4. Pull gathers to fit from one end of the lower jacket to the opposite end.
5. Beginning ½" from the top edge, right sides together, sandwich the ruffle between two lower pieces and pin in place.
6. Sew from one end to the opposite. Trim seam and finish.
7. Turn right-side out. Press.
8. Topstitch.
9. Run two lines of gathering stitches along the top edge of the lower coat.

To pull the gathers easily, break up the gathering stitches at each section.

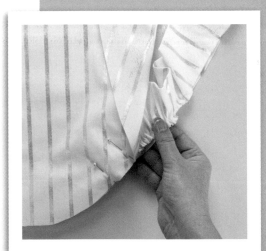

Step 5

Sewing the Curved Seams

1. Lay the coat top completely flat, wrong side facing up. Place the Curve C guide along the back sleeve stitch line, and draw a line along the curve. Repeat for the opposite side of the back.
2. Measure and mark ½" in from this line at the seam line.
3. Right sides together, fold along these lines and pin, narrowing to even with the seam line at the upper end.
4. Sew along this line. Repeat for the opposite side. Press.

Sewing the Sleeve Ruffles

1. Press under ¼" along one side of the sleeve ruffles.

2. Press under ½" again for the hem.

3. Topstitch.

4. Sew two rows of gathering stitches along the opposite sides at ⅛" and ¼".

5. Pull the gathers to fit the lower edge of the sleeve. Pin to the sleeve end, right sides together.

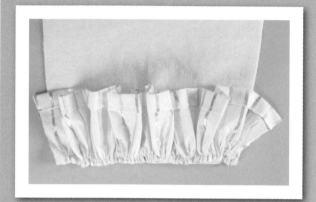

Step 6

6. Sew. Finish and press.

7. Topstitch along the sleeve edge, stitching narrow trim in place.

Sewing the Upper Coat

1. Sew two ruffle pieces together, end to end.

2. Fold in half right, sides together, and sew across the opposite ends. Trim and press.

3. Fold the entire piece in half, wrong sides together, and run two lines of gathering stitches.

4. Pull the gathers from one end of the upper coat to the opposite end to fit.

Step 5

5. Beginning ½" up from the edge, right sides together, pin the ruffle to the front edge from one edge to the other, leaving a ½" allowance.

6. Sew from one end to the opposite. Trim seam and finish.

7. Pin satin ribbon over the top of the seam on the inside. Topstitch in place.

Sewing the Side Seams

1. Fold the upper coat, right sides together, along the underarm seam line.

2. Sew seams. Finish and press.

3. Sew two lines of gathering stitches along the back edge between side seams.

Finishing the Coat

1. Pull gathers 2" in at the back of the upper coat.

2. Right sides together, pin the lower coat to the upper coat, beginning at the opposite front ends. Pin each front as far as the upper side seams.

3. Pull the gathers in the lower coat to fit the gathered upper coat. Pin.

4. Sew seam. Finish and press. Topstitch.

5. Tack the finished ends of the coat together with small stitches on the inside.

6. Fold the curved front flat, and mark snap placement on the inside. Sew in place.

Sewing the Ribbon Embroidery Roses

1. Cut an 18" length of ribbon. Thread a crewel needle with the ribbon.

> To maximize use of the ribbon before threading, take the point of the needle through the end of the ribbon. This will hold the ribbon in place.

2. Thread another needle with two strands of matching floss. Sew a straight stitch in the shape of a star on the garment. Each stitch should be approximately ½" long.

3. Knot a ribbon at the back of the star. Bring the ribbon up, and loop it in and out through the star. Twisted ribbon will add to the rose. Pull the ribbon gently.

4. Continue until the rose is finished, adding more ribbon from the back if needed.

Sewing the Belt

> A stripe was used for this jacket, so the belt was cut on the vertical into four pieces for visual interest. If you use a different pattern, cut the belt into two pieces the width of the fabric, trimming 2" off each end.

1. Sew the belt pieces right sides together and end to end, matching the stripe with a ½" seam. Finish and press.

2. Fold in half lengthwise, right sides together.

Step 3

3. Create a diagonal at the belt ends by folding the ends back even with the edge. Cut along the diagonal line.

4. Sew a seam along the raw edge, leaving a 2" opening in the center of the belt to turn.

5. Clip corners. Turn and press.

6. Topstitch around all four sides. Press.

7. Cut two 4" pieces of ribbon trim for belt loops. Fold the ends under ¼", and pin at the side seams of the coat, centering them between the upper and lower coat. Sew in place from the wrong side.

ACCENT, ALTER AND ACCESSORIZE!

Look for construction details or accessories that create a vertical line on the white, like a long jacket or duster, a long strand of beads, a long scarf, or a flattering, diagonal belt with a long chain or fringe. Verticals draw the eyes up and down instead of from side-to-side.

— Diana

Accent

- Add rhinestone buttons to the top of the sleeve.

- Embroider a similar stripe design with silver on the top of the coat.

- Add silver cording along the ruffle.

Alter

- Change colors: Try using white with a black satin ruffle and belt.

- Shorten or lengthen the coat for height. It can be shortened to the hip line.

- For a fuller bust, lengthen the top of the coat and use a darker color on top.

- For more width in the lower coat, cut separate front and back pieces. Refer to "The Accent is on You!" Chapter Two.

Accessorize!

- Silk-tie blouse

- White crepe pants

- Silver slingbacks

- Evening bag

- Silver filigree earrings

PATTERN SHEETS INDEX AND PROJECT NUMBERS

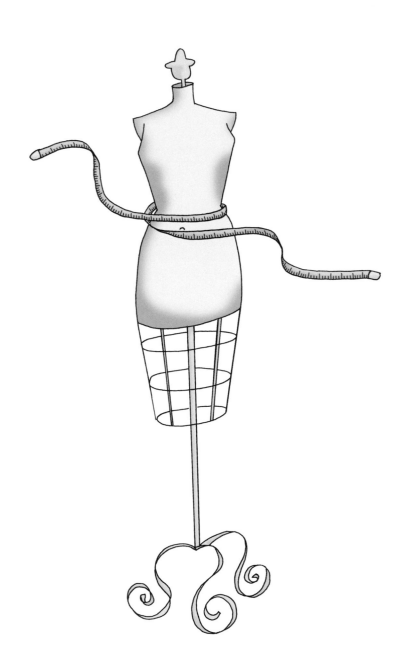

#1 THE ACCENT IS ON YOU!

#2 TROPICAL TEAL

#3 POLKA DOT PIZZAZZ

#4 A TOUCH OF THE ORIENT

#5 CELEBRATION OF CONTRASTS

#6 IN VESTED STYLE

#7 OH SEW BLUE

#8 FRESH AND FEMININE

#9 ATTITUDE PLUS

#10 FOR THE ANIMAL IN YOU!

#11 PETITE PLAY

#12 FALL FIESTA

#13 SNOWFLAKE SURPRISE!

#14 A LITTLE PINK

#15 HOLIDAY CHEER

#16 SILVER SHIMMER

#17 VAVOOM!

#18 CELESTIAL CHARM

#19 CRYSTAL CHANDELIER

SOURCE INFORMATION

Support your local craft and fabric retailers. If you are unable to find a particular product, contact the manufacturer to locate a store or mail-order source.

Beadalon
www.beadalon.com
1-800-423-2325
Beads

Caron International
www.caron.com
Variety of yarns, including Tigereye 0005 and Fire Agate 0021

Clover USA
www.clover-usa.com
Mini Iron

Coats & Clark
www.coatsandclark.com
1-800-648-1479
Embroidery floss

Expo International
www.expointl.com
1-800-542-4367
Beaded trims

Fiskars
www.fiskars.com
Scissors, rotary cutter,
self-healing mat, ruler

Kandi Corp.
1-727-726-6099
www.kandicorp.com
Crystal Crafter Applicator,
Iron-on crystals and studs

Kreinik Manufacturing Co., Inc.
www.kreinik.com
1-800-537-2166
Iron-on- metallic braids

Offray Ribbon
1-800-344-5533
Satin ribbon

Plaid
www.plaidonline.com
Royal Coat Decoupage Medium

Therm O Web
www.thermoweb.com
HeatnBond Iron-on Adhesive

ILLUSTRATOR
DEBORAH PEYTON

Deborah Peyton is a well-known Canadian cartoonist and illustrator. Her Fine-Tooning business has published books, as well as a daily cartoon series in several Canadian and US newspapers. She also has created many illustrations for textbooks and promotional materials, and developed original characters for several programs. Humorous greeting cards and clever caricatures showcase her varied talents as well. At present, much of her work is in creating wonderful artwork and illustrations for books, including several for Krause Publications: "Easy-to-Sew Playful Toys," "Contemporary Machine-Embroidered Fashions," and "Contemporary Machine-Embroidered Accessories." Deborah is a member of the National Cartoonists Society.

Deborah also has joined with author and designer Debra Quartermain in a partnership to develop artwork concepts for licensing, PQexpressions!. The partnership has had two baby quilting fabric lines released by Northcott, based on toys from the "Easy-to-Sew Playful Toys," and both members are constantly working on new ideas for their next project. As partners and great friends, working together is busy but always fun. Especially when it involves a working lunch over coconut cream pie!.

Deborah shares her home in the beautiful countryside of New Brunswick, Canada, just outside the village of New Maryland with her husband, two daughters, chickens, cats, a dog and horses.

More about Deborah and her portfolio can be seen at www.pqexpressions.com.

IMAGE CONSULTANT DIANA PEMBERTON-SIKES

A former model and unrepentant clotheshorse, Diana Pemberton-Sikes is a certified color and image consultant who has been helping women reach their image goals since 1994.

Since starting the FashionForRealWomen.com Web site in 2000, Diana has been featured in dozens of magazines, including Women's World, Weight Watchers, Paris Woman, and The American Bar Association, on ContentBiz.com, and in numerous fashion and beauty e-zines all over the web.

You can also find her "words of wisdom" in Priscilla Y. Huff's, "The Self-Employed Woman's Guide to Launching a Home-Based Business" and in "FabJob Guide To Become a Fashion Designer."

ABOUT THE AUTHOR

Author and designer Debra Quartermain combines her talent and love of inspiring creativity by designing stylish wearables, whimsical soft toys and sophisticated home decor items. Her designs have been featured in magazines such as Bead Unique, Crafts 'n Things, Country Marketplace, Create and Decorate, Today's Creative Home Arts and PaperCrafts. Debra has authored four books and collaborated on several others. Her books include "Nursery Decor," "Easy-to-Sew Playful Toys" and "Sweatshirts," published by Krause Publications.

Debra also works with manufacturers to produce designs and instructions for their products. As a speaker, Debra offers an informative and entertaining presentation sharing her love of creativity. She is a current member of CHA and was on the SCD Board.

As a licensed designer, Debra has designed patterns for Butterick/McCalls and at present is in a partnership, PQexpressions!, with Deborah Peyton to develop fabric lines for the quilting industry. The first two baby lines are based on toys from "Easy to Sew Playful Toys," "Buggles" and "Wiggles 'n Giggles," manufactured and distributed across North America by Northcott Silk. Their partnership is filled with many late-night collaborations and working lunches amidst papers, pencils and coconut cream pie!

Debra creates and lives in a colorful, fabric-filled design studio in the pretty village of New Maryland in New Brunswick, Canada with daughters, cats, good friends and a beautiful Samoyed, Cleo, always nearby.

Visit www.pqexpressions to view Debra's portfolio. Visit her blog, "The (not so) Secret Confessions of a Stitch Chick," at www.debraquartermain.typepad.com/confessionsofastitchchick for a light-hearted look at life in the creative sewing lane!

...and they all were worn happily ever after.

The End!

(of course not; its just the beginning of fabulous jackets!)

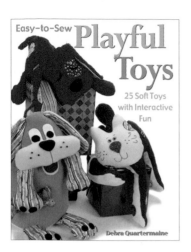

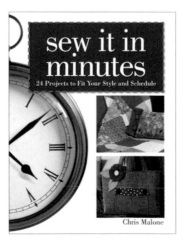